POWER OF THE MIND
IN HEALTH AND HEALING

KEITH R. HOLDEN, M.D.

POWER OF THE MIND IN HEALTH AND HEALING

Copyright © **2016 Keith R. Holden, M.D.**

All rights reserved.

Published by **WaveCloud Corporation 2016**

Websites: www.Dr-Holden.com

www.mindinhealing.com

ISBN: 978-1-5356-0161-0

I dedicate this book with love to Mike, Mom, Dad, Dianne, Nataya, John, Ray, Brenda, Judith, Heather, Cathy, and Kevin. Your unconditional love and support has encouraged and inspired me to be authentic and speak my truth. I'll always be thankful for each of you.

Contents

Introduction

THE PURPOSE OF THIS BOOK is to educate and inspire you to work with your mind to improve your health and your life. It includes some of the latest research on mind-body medicine and emphasizes real-world applications of these findings.

I take you on a journey of mind-body mastery starting with the basics of mindfulness and meditation. Then I show you how to work with your subconscious mind to remove limiting beliefs and release negative emotions. I also teach you how to hack the placebo effect to take advantage of the power of belief and optimize your health.

Some of this information is cutting-edge science, and a smaller part is philosophical. I include philosophy because science can't explain the spiritual aspect of the human experience. I include spirituality because it is at the merger of science and spirituality where we'll make some of mankind's greatest discoveries. Spirituality can only be defined by your personal and unique experiences with a loving force that permeates our universe.

As you read this book, use healthy skepticism and let yourself consider possibilities you might not have thought about before. Your mind is the most powerful thing in your control. By using the mind-body techniques taught in this book, you'll discover some amazing super powers you didn't know you had.

Do not use the information in this book as a substitute for care by a licensed healthcare practitioner.

In this book, you'll learn:

- The fascinating science that proves why mind-body medicine is so powerful.
- Simple techniques and processes for beginning and maintaining a mindfulness and meditation practice.
- Easy mind-body techniques to quickly and effectively relax and turn off your stress response.
- Simple mindfulness techniques for healthier eating.
- How to maximize present-moment awareness to magnify creativity and manifestation.
- How to effectively change your perception so that you experience less stress.
- How to use a heart-centered meditation to diffuse any negative emotion.
- How to maximize your intuition through meditation, and the science behind it.
- How to use brainwave entrainment technology to deepen your meditative states.
- How to uncover limiting beliefs stuck in your subconscious mind and use a specific guided meditation technique to remove them.

- The effective use of core positive affirmations and how to bypass any mental blocks around them.
- Basic functional medicine concepts for building a strong body and mind.
- Functional medicine nutritional support advice.
- How the science behind the placebo effect proves your unlimited ability to heal yourself, and how to maximize this power in your everyday life.
- How to activate your inner physician to trigger a biological cascade of events for self-healing.
- How to tap into your higher mind — higher self — to know the truth and become your own authority.

This book includes access to six guided meditations that are integral to the application of its concepts. To download these meditations, go to www.mindinhealing.com/guided-meditations.

Each guided meditation contains a specific intention to optimize the power of your mind with the ultimate goal of improving your health. Brainwave entrainment tracks are embedded in each guided meditation recording to help trigger your relaxation response. I recommend you listen to the guided meditations in a quiet place, using earphones or earbuds to get the best effect.

The guided meditations become more advanced as the book progresses. It's important that you master the basics of mindfulness and meditation before progressing to the advanced meditation techniques. These basics include diaphragmatic breathing (belly breathing), fully engaging the present moment, and triggering a sustained relaxation response. Don't worry — it's easy. I'll walk you through learning the basics.

As a teaching technique in this book, I use a fair amount of repetition of core concepts, and I do so for two reasons: repetition helps the brain memorize, and these core concepts are integral to your success with the techniques I teach.

My favorite internal medicine professor once said, "If you throw enough sh*t on the barnyard wall, some of it will start to stick." He was one of the best teachers I've ever had and he used repetition of important points to help his residents learn complex topics. Some of the concepts I present are a little complex for the non-medical layperson, though I did my best to simplify them. I still felt it was necessary to use repetition in this book to help you learn them.

You'll see that the core concepts repeat throughout the different chapters of the book because they build on one another to create the bigger picture. Forgive me if you feel there is too much repetition, but I think you'll appreciate the style. I do try to use a different type of wording with the repetition, because sometimes when you hear something again, but in a slightly different way, it finally makes sense.

Preface

To help you better understand my background and inspiration for writing this book, I'd like to share a personal story.

I was born a twin to loving parents in a small town in Louisiana. We were large twins and cramped in utero. This resulted in my twin needing to wear corrective shoes with braces. I was born with a crossed eye and a weak neck resulting in my head tending to rest on one shoulder. My parents immediately took me to our family chiropractor. In 1964, the traditional medical establishment considered chiropractors quacks. As I've come to learn, a healer is a healer. My eye uncrossed, and my neck became strong enough to hold up my head after Dr. Eastman adjusted my tiny body. Dr. Eastman is a hero to me — a true pioneer in the art of medicine. He bravely faced prejudice by a powerful medical institution that attempted to squash his profession.

In 1966, the American Medical Association (AMA) adopted a resolution calling the chiropractic profession an "unscientific cult," and in 1967, issued an official opinion making it unethical for physicians to associate with chiropractors. In 1976, a few chiropractors filed an antitrust lawsuit against the AMA, charging restraint of trade, and in 1987, a federal judge found the AMA guilty of conspiring to destroy chiropractic. In 1990, the court of appeals found the AMA guilty, and later in 1990, the US Supreme Court upheld the earlier legal findings. Finally, in 1992, the AMA reached a settlement with the plaintiffs, requiring the AMA to complete all of the terms of the court order.

My experience with Dr. Eastman was the first of many healing experiences facilitated by alternative medicine practitioners. I have reflected upon that experience each time I came across prejudice against alternative forms of medicine. My story of healing through nontraditional means at an early age has become a guidepost for me. It has reminded me to keep an open mind about nontraditional therapeutic methods. Keeping an open mind has been a gift, helping me become a better practitioner of the art of medicine.

I've come to realize just how sensitive a child I was. I remember my mother trying to soothe me back to sleep after recurring bad dreams. In kindergarten, I remember crying for my father not to leave when he dropped me off at school. I wasn't interested in hunting animals like my other brothers, but went hunting with them as a way to fit in. I was bullied in sixth, seventh, and tenth grades, possibly because I was perceived as weak due to my sensitivity. In retrospect, I've learned that highly sensitive children have an abundance of compassion and empathy. Parents can support these children by focusing on acceptance of this sensitivity and seeing it as a gift.

I always had a nervous stomach in my childhood. This was especially true when eating out with my family at restaurants. I'd come to learn that my nervousness about eating was linked to an overactive sympathetic nervous system. This state of "fight-or-flight" interfered with normal digestion. It also helped set me up later in life for a severe gastrointestinal disorder.

I loved medical school and my internal medicine residency. I thrived in a structured educational environment and craved intellectual stimulation. I graduated from medical school as a junior-year member of the Alpha Omega Honor Medical Society. This honor is reserved for the top ten percent of medical school classes. When I graduated from residency and started practicing primary care, my passion for medicine began to wane. Part of my discontent was boredom. I was seeing lots of head colds, stomach viruses, and back pain, which is typical for a primary care doctor.

The most prominent player in my discontent was the dogmatic way I was expected to practice medicine. My training in medical school and residency was indoctrination into a certain mindset, which included a belief that any healing methods outside of the box hinged upon malpractice. This created an internal conflict for me that I couldn't shake. After all, I had already experienced an alternative healing method that had actually worked.

I was seeing many patients who didn't get well despite following the best evidence-based medicine (EBM). I found this dogmatic approach to practicing medicine stifling and sometimes harmful to patients. If a patient has multiple diseases, EBM sometimes calls for them to be on up to eight or ten medications at once. Sometimes I'd have to address the side effects of medications with, guess what, more medications. In some patients, EBM creates a vicious cycle of dangerous polypharmacy. This wasn't what I had envisioned the practice of medicine would be.

Then came a horrible blow. One year out of residency, a patient sued me for malpractice. I was devastated. I always prided myself on ordering the right tests and making the correct diagnosis. My physician assistant had injected a patient's Achilles tendon, resulting in the tendon rupturing. We were both named in the lawsuit, as well as the clinic I worked for at the time. From that point on, I became extra vigilant and practiced defensive medicine. This hypervigilance exacerbated my underlying propensity for fight-or-flight. Every time I saw a patient after that, the interaction was tainted by the fear that I would be sued again. I couldn't shake this fear, and it created a form of posttraumatic stress disorder.

The lawsuit dragged on for five years, and I underwent multiple depositions. Some of the depositions were lessons in how to remain calm while undergoing a personal attack on my integrity. As I was packing my suitcase to travel to Louisiana to go to a jury trial, I got a call from my attorney. He told me that I had been dropped from the lawsuit, and the clinic had settled the claim for a small amount of money. I was relieved, but the experience left me with an unease that has taken thirteen years to shed.

I went on with my life and the practice of internal medicine, but in the back of my mind I was looking for a way out. I began working part-time, helping case managers adjudicate Social Security disability claims. I excelled in this field, because I was good at collating complex information into concise summaries. I also didn't have the stress of seeing patients in this arena. I later left the practice of medicine and did this full-time for several years. I came back to internal medicine out of sheer boredom. I missed the healing arts, and it was time for me to recertify in internal medicine. I returned to my old practice and put my nose to the grindstone. I began seeing patients while working on certification modules and studying for my board test.

I also began studying the alternative healing arts. If I was going to stay in medicine, I was going to do it differently this time. I could not go back and do the same old thing that had led to my dissatisfaction in the first place. I passed my board test and recertified in internal medicine. I decided I was going to use these credentials to establish my own practice. This time, I was going to do it my way.

It was about this time that I came across The Institute of Functional Medicine. Their courses teach functional medicine, which is essentially science-based American naturopathy. As I began to learn the concepts, at first, I became angry. The information I was learning filled in the blanks medical school and residency left out. Why wasn't I taught this in medical school? It would have made such a difference in the lives of my patients. It's the same reasons the AMA tried to squash chiropractic — bias, academic arrogance, and shortsightedness.

The traditional medical model does well treating acute injury and illness but not so well treating chronic illness. This is where functional medicine excels. A major obstacle in bringing functional medicine mainstream is that many insurance companies won't pay for it. It also requires practitioners to spend quality time with their patients. Insurance companies won't adequately pay for that either.

About the time I found functional medicine, I also discovered electroceuticals. Electroceuticals are energy-based devices that are making a comeback into mainstream medicine. Some examples include pulsed electromagnetic-field devices, microcurrent devices, and vagus nerve stimulators. I adopted a pulsed electromagnetic-field device and a microcurrent device into my practice with amazing results. Physicians used electroceuticals in the early 1900s, but passage of the Flexner Report in 1910 banished these devices and ushered in a new era of medical education.

So life was good again. I began practicing as a functional medicine specialist in a cash-based practice. I was using some effective electroceutical devices. Then life threw me another curve ball. I decided to have all my dental fillings removed after having read about the risk of mercury toxicity. In my haste, I did not adequately prepare, and asked my dentist to remove all seven in one day. This turned out to be a big mistake.

Less than one month after their removal, my stomach swelled like I was six months pregnant. No matter what I did,

I could not get rid of the bloating. Shortly after that, I started having diarrhea and weight loss. After losing ten pounds over several months, I became very scared. In addition, severe bouts of anxiety set in. While getting ready for work some mornings, intense anxiousness would wash over me. I'd start having intensely worried thoughts followed by what seemed like someone turning on a water faucet under my armpits. Some mornings I was so drenched in sweat that I would have to take another shower.

I saw a gastroenterologist and underwent an upper and lower endoscopy. The upper endoscopy was normal, but the colonoscopy showed aphthous ulcers scattered throughout my sigmoid colon. Biopsies were consistent with aphthous ulcers and not Crohn's disease or ulcerative colitis. My gastroenterologist prescribed a well-known drug used to treat inflammatory bowel disease (IBD). A few days later, I flew out of state. That night on October 10, 2010, I became the sickest I've ever been in my entire life. I developed constant diarrhea with abdominal cramps so bad the only thing that gave me relief was lying submerged in warm water. So I lay in a warm bathtub for almost twenty-four hours on the first day of my vacation.

I didn't want to go to a hospital out of state, so I called my gastroenterologist. She prescribed Questran powder, and I began taking it. In about four hours, my symptoms started to subside. She called to check on me and told me to stop the IBD drug because in some individuals it can exacerbate IBD. How ironic — a drug used to treat a condition can cause worsening of the condition, which is actually not a rarity. I decided I wasn't going to take any more medications for this condition since the medication had made me drastically worse. There had to be another way.

I returned home and began experiencing fatigue so bad that I was only able to see a few patients a day. I'd often come home and take a nap at lunchtime just to be able to get through the rest of the day. Some Saturdays were spent on the couch, recovering from the week. When I'd make it to the gym, my muscles would ache like the worst case of post-workout muscle soreness. I was no longer able to hold a chiropractic adjustment for more than a few days. My body would frequently torque, causing one shoulder or one hip to be higher than the other. I'd also get intense spasms in my neck and upper back causing terrible tension headaches.

Then I began waking up in the middle of the night with intense hunger. I'd need to get up and eat before I could go back to sleep. Sometimes when I'd stand up suddenly, I'd have to sit back down because of dizziness caused by low blood pressure. These symptoms were due to adrenal fatigue and mitochondrial dysfunction. The scariest part was when I'd develop severe palpitations when drinking cold water. I'd have to lie down and perform a Valsalva maneuver before the palpitations would stop. When I'd check my pulse during these episodes, it felt irregular at a rate of about 140. This was consistent with atrial fibrillation. My body was in chaos.

I ordered labs on myself and underwent a computed tomography (CT) scan of my chest and abdomen. Heartburn was so severe it would cause difficulty swallowing at times. The chest CT was normal, and the abdominal CT only showed a benign hemangioma in my liver. My relief was short-lived, as the weight loss continued despite eating five thousand calories a day. Something was terribly wrong, and I thought I was going to die. I tried every functional medicine trick in the book and nothing seemed to help. I know what you are thinking — doctors should never treat themselves. I agree. But after my bad experience with the medication, I was wary of seeing traditional doctors.

I saw an alternative medicine physician who diagnosed me with mercury toxicity. He told me that my body had been bordering on the brink of disaster due to multiple precursors. The most prominent was my longstanding poorly managed stress. Years of discontent, hypervigilance, and emotional hypersensitivity also played a role. These combined with my genetic aberrancies created a tipping point when I was exposed to the excess mercury.

My body had been accumulating mercury over the years from the environment, eating tuna, and mercury leaching from my amalgams. The significant exposure during the removal of my amalgams was the final straw. My weakest link — my gut — was poisoned and went into chaos.

There were several other contributors to this disaster. I struggled with severe acne in high school and college, for which I took multiple rounds of antibiotics. The antibiotics wiped out my healthy gut microbiome, causing immune dysfunction, leaky gut, and yeast overgrowth. The physician explained to me that, depending on each person's unique genetic makeup, some are good detoxifiers of mercury, and some are not. A homozygous methylation defect plus other single nucleotide polymorphisms (SNPs) contributed to my inability to detoxify mercury well. These revelations finally put the pieces of the puzzle together.

He prescribed a mercury chelation regimen including injections of DMPS, a powerful mercury chelator. He warned me that because of my weakened system, I might experience intense side effects. I didn't care at that point because I was already miserable and had tried so much else. Shortly after I began the DMPS injections, I experienced bouts of bloody diarrhea and worsening fatigue. I continued the medication this time, knowing it was getting to the true root of the problem. Thankfully, after a couple of weeks, things began to improve. The DMPS injections helped me finally turn the corner by eliminating mercury from my body. My gut came back online, and I began gaining weight.

It's been four years since my gut started functioning with some semblance of normalcy. It's been a long and slow process of recovery. Only in the past month has the constant bloating stopped. My energy is much better, and I've put on five pounds of muscle in the past nine months.

A key to my recovery is the consistent practice of mindfulness and meditation. This practice helps keep my perceived level of stress low. I say perceived because it's always a perception that creates an emotional stress response. Mindfulness and meditation balance my excessive sensitivity by helping me create a perception filter. Slowing down and paying attention to the present moment enhances this filter. This reduces the onslaught of overwhelming sensory stimuli and keeps me from catastrophizing. A regular meditation practice has honed my ability to stay fully present and calm in the midst of chaos.

Regularly meditating on trust has helped me to stay trustful about my life's experiences. Before, I would fall into a victim's role, which is completely disempowering. If I do start to feel disempowered, the feeling doesn't last long. This is because I've created deep neuronal pathways of trust in my brain through regular meditation. Meditation has strengthened my ability to tap into a deeper knowing about my life's experiences. This lets me more easily find the path of least resistance.

I'm telling my story of recovery despite feeling vulnerable, because I want you to know that things will get better, no matter how tough life seems. Getting better requires that you establish a state of mind of peace, patience, and trust. This type of mindset leads to self-confidence and a sense of empowerment, which leads to your life getting better. These attributes are easier to achieve through a regular practice of mindfulness and meditation. So stick with your practices and never forget — you can do it. You are all-powerful.

Chapter 1
Consciousness and Physical Correlates

Consciousness is an energy pervading the universe, making it aware of itself.
— Keith R. Holden, MD

THIS INFOGRAPHIC PROVIDES A VISUAL representation of how the mind, or consciousness, impacts the physical body. What follows is a brief description of each section in the graph to help you understand some of the main points of this book.

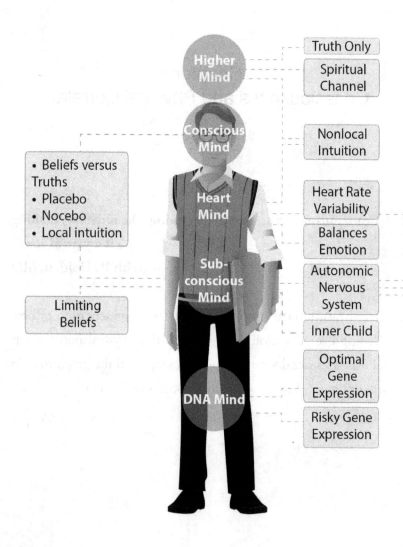

Figure 1: *Consciousness and Physical Correlates*

Sympathetic
Nervous System

Parasympathetic
Nervous System

- Stress Response
- Fight or Flight
- Accelerator on

- Immobilization Response
- Numbness & Disscociation
- Dorsal Vagal - Freeze & Fold
- Hand brake & Accelerator on

- Relaxation Response
- Rest & Digest
- Foot brake on

Higher Mind

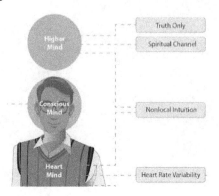

Figure 2: *Higher Mind*

Some call the higher mind the higher self or soul self. It is literally a spiritual channel and only knows the truth. Your higher mind is an energetic aspect of you that projects out of your physical body like an antenna and connects you with the unified field of energy.

The unified field of energy is what scientists are hoping to explain one day by a Unified Field Theory. Scientists are searching for all the energy particles in our universe with a goal of creating a mathematical model for the Unified Field Theory. They use tools like the Large Hadron Collider in Europe to discover these energy particles. The unified field consists of energies connecting everyone and everything, including the spiritual realm with the earth plane.

Your higher mind is the part of your consciousness that you tap into when doing spiritual-type practices. But you don't have to consider yourself spiritual to tap into this aspect of your consciousness. You may even consider yourself an atheist, and it still works quite well. This is because our universe is based on energy, and your higher mind is simply energy. It doesn't care whether you believe in it or not, though belief in it may create resonance in energy fields to help optimize its function.

Some people have a personal bias against terms describing anything religious or spiritual. When I use the terms "spirituality" and "divine," I'm referencing universal energies unexplained by science. These universal energies are available to us to help facilitate our paths in life.

Nonlocal versus Local Intuition

I make a distinct connection of your higher mind with your heart mind in this infographic. That's because there is scientific evidence, which I detail later, that shows your higher mind channels nonlocal intuitive information to your heart mind.

Nonlocal intuition comes from an unexplained knowing. It has nothing to do with pattern recognition or memory retrieval. In contrast, local intuition originates in your conscious and subconscious minds and is derived from the brain functions of pattern recognition and memory retrieval. Local intuition is the type of intuition the traditional scientific model studies. These traditional researchers say your conscious mind and subconscious mind work together to bring up forgotten memories and see patterns to help you intuit something.

Pioneering researchers of mind-body medicine and psi phenomena study nonlocal intuition. These scientists include Dean Radin, PhD of the Institute of Noetic Sciences, and

Rollin McCraty, PhD at the Institute of HeartMath. They study nonlocal intuition to help explain the vast complexity of consciousness.

Dean Radin, PhD says, "The idea of the universe as an interconnected whole is not new; for millennia it's been one of the core assumptions of Eastern philosophies. What is new is that Western science is slowly beginning to realize that some elements of that ancient lore might be correct."

Heart Mind

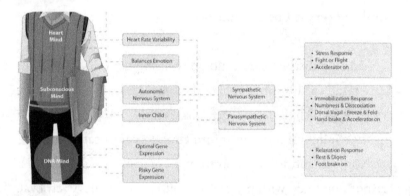

Figure 3: *Heart Mind*

The heart mind is the consciousness of your heart. It is one of the most powerful aspects of your being because it contains the wisdom of unconditional love.

The HeartMath Institute has been performing cutting-edge mind-body research since 1991. Their research emphasizes the heart-mind connection. They've developed innovative tools that help people all over the world connect their hearts and minds.

They understand that the heart has an incredibly powerful innate intelligence. HeartMath has published numerous studies in peer-reviewed medical journals showing the power of heart consciousness.

Their research emphasizes heart rate variability, which is the beat-to-beat variation of your heart rhythm. They show how heart rate variability helps measure the heart-mind connection.

Another important point they make in their research is that the heart has its own brain. Think about it. Surgeons cut the vagus nerve and spinal nerves during a heart transplant. These are nerves that help regulate the heart's functions. Despite severing these nerves, the transplanted heart functions quite well.

This proves that the heart has an independently functioning brain and nervous system. This independently functioning nervous system, combined with the consciousness of the heart, is what I call your heart mind. Your heart mind contains not only physical but also emotional and spiritual components as well.

Having a heart-centered life and engaging people with your heart are references to the heart's consciousness. In fact, your entire body is conscious, which is why all its parts communicate so fast and so efficiently.

Research by the HeartMath Institute suggests that your heart mind is the first part of your consciousness to receive nonlocal intuitive information. This nonlocal intuitive information is coming from outside of your physical body from the unified field of energy that connects everyone and everything. Your heart mind then transmits that information to your conscious mind. I go into that study in detail later in the book.

The HeartMath Institute has designed devices containing software to measure heart rate variability. Measuring of heart rate variability is useful because it reflects back to you the balance of your autonomic nervous system. This biofeedback shows you how well your mindfulness and meditation practices are balancing your autonomic nervous system. Your autonomic nervous system is on autopilot and is responsible for your body's functions that you're not consciously regulating. These functions include heart rate, blood pressure, sweating, temperature regulation, and digestion.

Autonomic Nervous System

Your autonomic nervous system has two main parts — sympathetic and parasympathetic. The sympathetic nervous system controls your fight-or-flight stress response. The parasympathetic nervous system controls your rest-and-digest relaxation response.

Mindfulness and meditation trigger your relaxation response to help balance your autonomic nervous system. Many people are in a chronic stress response due to worrying about families, jobs, and finances. This chronic stress response causes an overactive sympathetic nervous system, which creates an imbalance in your autonomic nervous system. Mindfulness, meditation, and diaphragmatic breathing reduce stress and trigger your relaxation response. This results in less sympathetic nervous system activity and more parasympathetic nervous system activity. The result is a balanced autonomic nervous system.

Prolonged stress causes excessive sympathetic nervous system activity, which breaks down your body's systems. Prolonged stress causes and worsens illness and disease. Mindfulness, meditation, and diaphragmatic breathing help prevent disease by balancing your autonomic nervous system.

Immobilization Response

An immobilization response to stress is a pathologic mixture of the sympathetic and parasympathetic response. An immobilization response relates to psychological numbness and dissociation. It's like pressing on the accelerator of a car while setting the handbrake. Here is an example of the immobilization response. A fire breaks out on your airplane while it sits on the tarmac. Even though you know you should get up and move to the nearest exit, you remain frozen in your seat.

Training your body-mind with mindfulness, meditation, and diaphragmatic breathing balances your autonomic nervous system. A balanced autonomic nervous system helps reduce your chances of experiencing an immobilization response to stress.

Balancing Emotions with Your Heart Mind

You can use the consciousness of your heart to balance your emotions. This is because your heart mind contains the high-energy emotion of unconditional love. You can tap into this high-energy emotion to transmute and balance low-energy emotions like anger and shame. I walk you through that technique later in the book.

Conscious Mind and Subconscious Mind

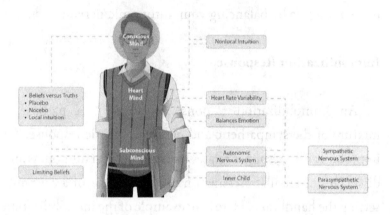

Figure 4: Conscious Mind and Subconscious Mind

Your conscious mind is highly analytical and can easily get you into trouble. Excessive thinking or rumination can trigger your stress response. This is especially true when ruminating on worry and other types of fearful thinking.

Your subconscious mind correlates with your autonomic nervous system, and both are running on autopilot. Your subconscious mind contains the part of your consciousness that helps regulate this autopilot. Many of us have beliefs stuck in our subconscious minds that we aren't aware of. These include limiting beliefs originating in childhood. Later in the book, I describe an effective technique for removing limiting beliefs.

Beliefs versus Truths

The concept of "beliefs versus truths" holds that not every belief is a truth, despite having the belief. You can learn to discern the truth about your beliefs through a healthy integration of your conscious and subconscious minds. Later, I teach you a method for discerning the truth.

Placebo and Nocebo Effect

The intersection of your conscious and subconscious minds is where the placebo and nocebo effect occurs. The latest research on the placebo effect is mind-boggling. It shows that the power of belief influences your physiology in amazing ways. Later, I simplify this research and show you how to apply these findings to improve your health.

Limiting Beliefs

Your subconscious mind contains limiting beliefs. These are beliefs embedded deeply in your subconscious that limit you in some way. Most of these are lies you bought into in childhood that became part of your belief system. These beliefs act like a virus, infecting your mind with untruths. Most of the time, you're not even aware they exist. Your subconscious mind is always filtering your experiences. You can't always see the truth in your experiences because limiting beliefs muddy this subconscious filter.

DNA Mind

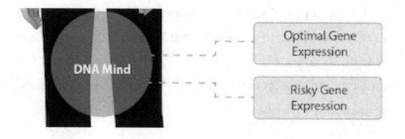

Figure 5: DNA Mind

Your DNA mind is the consciousness that permeates your DNA. Your DNA contains the genetic blueprint for your body-mind. Your thoughts can trigger changes in your DNA to turn genes on and off. Later, I discuss research showing how mindfulness and meditation improve health by turning genes on and off. By changing your thoughts to trigger a relaxation response, you change how your genes express. This results in less body rust, less inflammation, and improved energy. It also has an anti-aging effect by preserving the ends of chromosomes called telomeres. This emphasizes the power of your mind to change how your genes express to improve your health.

Chapter 2
Mindfulness and Meditation

MINDFULNESS AND MEDITATION ARE POWERFUL mind-body practices. These practices involve paying attention to the present moment without judgment. Another description of these practices is to watch, witness, and allow.

"Without judgment" involves witnessing your experience with a higher awareness. In doing so, you don't create a state of resistance to what is. This works by invoking a curiosity about the experience rather than judging the experience. When you maintain this higher awareness, you can still decide to make changes. It just won't trigger a stress response.

Resistance to "what is" triggers a stress response and pulls you into a state of intense reactivity. This may be necessary for jumping out of the way of a moving car. But in situations that aren't life threatening, this may block your ability to see all of your options for changing the situation.

Using mindfulness and meditation to create states of nonresistance about stress requires proper context. There are appropriate times to be in a state of nonresistance to what is. Use mindfulness and meditation to create states of nonresistance in situations that do not put you in immediate danger. Ultimately, it's about creating a balance between overreacting and efficient responses.

Mindfulness and meditation get a lot of press these days. More and more research shows these practices have multiple health benefits, which I'll detail shortly. Peer-reviewed scientific literature uses the terms mindfulness, meditation, and mindfulness meditation interchangeably. There are various definitions for each term, but the definitions aren't as important as what these processes can do for you. Practices and definitions surrounding these concepts have been passed down from the ancients. These concepts have been associated with everything from religions to the New Age movement. The phrase "New Age movement" is funny because these concepts involve old traditions and beliefs. Some say being mindful is a way of life — a practice of calmly engaging the present moment as often as you can. Others say that meditation is a subset of mindfulness where you calm your body-mind while narrowing your focus. There is a lot of overlap in these two concepts, depending on your goal for using them.

From a health perspective, a goal of mindfulness and meditation is to trigger your relaxation response. This means creating a state of relaxation in your body-mind. This relaxation response is the opposite of your stress response. Relaxation results in a cascade of positive physiologic events. This includes a reduction of stress hormones like cortisol, and balancing of your autonomic nervous system.

Your body begins to repair and heal when you increase your parasympathetic relaxation response. Your body-mind is an infinitely intelligent organism and knows how to heal itself when properly supported. A key factor in this automatic healing is a balanced autonomic nervous system.

According to the HeartMath Institute, coherence in heart rate variability reflects a balanced autonomic nervous system. Heart rate variability is the beat-to-beat variation in your heart rhythm, which is highly variable in healthy individuals. Mindfulness and meditation create coherence in your heart rate variability. This coherence is then propagated to all your body's organ systems. Body wide coherence results in optimal and efficient functioning of your entire body.

Using Your Breath as a Starting Place

An easy way to start with mindfulness and meditation is to simply focus on your breathing. You're always breathing but rarely ever thinking about it. So just use what you already have as a starting place. Set a timer for five minutes, get into a relaxed position, close your eyes, and start taking slow, relaxed, deep breaths, in and out.

It's a little more challenging than you might think. You will most likely find that your mind starts to wander to your to-do list or something else. When that happens, mindfully bring a relaxed focus back to your breath. Start with a goal of five minutes per day and work your way up from there.

The optimal way to breathe when you do a breath meditation is to belly breathe. This is also called diaphragmatic breathing. It requires that you actively engage your diaphragm. Diaphragmatic breathing helps improve oxygen flow to the rest of your body. It also triggers a relaxation response by stimulating your vagus nerve. You will know you are properly engaging your diaphragm when your abdomen extends outward when you take a deep breath in.

We all used to be really good at diaphragmatic breathing as babies. It's a healthier way to breathe because it triggers a relaxation response. Chest breathing is something we learned to do when stressed. Notice the next time you are stressed that you are breathing shallow with your chest, and not moving your abdomen.

Optimally, you want to do diaphragmatic breathing when doing a breath meditation. The good thing is that this simple technique results in numerous health benefits. In triggering your relaxation response, it balances your autonomic nervous system.

To view an instructional YouTube video on diaphragmatic or belly breathing, go to http://bit.ly/BellyBreathingVideo

To download the free Breathe2Relax app for Android or iOS platforms, go to http://bit.ly/Breathe2RelaxApp

Mindfulness Practices for Stress Reduction

You can practice mindfulness while sitting, standing, walking, or eating. All it takes is fully engaging the present moment in whatever you are doing. It's a skill you can easily master with a little practice. Most of us are really good at multitasking because we practice it often. When done in excess, multitasking results in you being mentally fatigued and less efficient. So the idea is to balance your multitasking with mindfulness.

When you first start practicing mindfulness, I recommend you use reminders to do it. These reminders let you be mindful of mindfulness. Set reminders with an alarm on your smartphone or computer. Also, paste sticky notes around your home or office to remind you to be mindful.

When cued, fully engage in the present moment for a few minutes. After a while, you will notice you instinctively remember to do this without external cues. You will have conditioned yourself to remember to be mindful. The goal is to balance your overthinking and multitasking by integrating periods of mindfulness.

Using Nature as a Cue

Use nature as a cue to practice mindfulness. When you step outside into nature, use this as a cue to fully engage in nature, even if just for a few seconds or minutes. When you go outside, or even when viewing nature through a window, become aware of your natural surroundings. The energy in nature is usually a pure and calming type of energy that soothes your autonomic nervous system. Think about how you felt the last time you took a walk in the woods or a walk on the beach.

Studies show that nature, and especially forests, positively impact your physiology. Exposure to forests even improves your immune system. (1, 2, 3) So take a good look at your natural surroundings. Consciously smell the fresh air. Feel the breeze on your skin. When walking to your car, become aware of nature so that you avoid going over a mental to-do list, or worrying about what's going to happen when you get to work or school.

Engaging nature resets your conscious mind by reminding you of the peacefulness in nature. This creates a relaxation response in your body-mind. The more you practice using nature as a cue for mindfulness, the easier it gets. Letting nature remind you to relax helps balance your autonomic nervous system.

Take walks in nature while focusing on the beauty in nature. Sit in nature while peacefully watching all that is in nature. The energies in nature will soothe you if you allow them into your life. It's a simple way to start practicing being mindful while at the same time engaging a naturally peaceful energy.

Grounding Visualization

Here is a practice that I do on a regular basis to get grounded. It's a combination of visual imagery and meditation. Stand on the earth in your bare feet. Close your eyes and visualize grounding yourself to the earth. See roots extending from the bottoms of your feet to the center of the earth. Take some slow, deep belly breaths, and imagine releasing all your fears and frustrations into the earth. I recommend you do this several times a week. This is a powerful meditation and you'll be surprised how it makes you feel.

To download the Feeling Grounded Guided Meditation, go to www.mindinhealing.com/guided-meditations.

Mindful Eating

Practice mindfulness when preparing a meal, and especially when eating. The main purpose of eating is to replenish your nutrients and support your body's metabolism. Maximize that by being mindful of this process. Many people use food as a way to self-medicate by eating comfort foods to make them feel better. Eating triggers a release of the neurotransmitters in your brain, including feel-good neurotransmitters. The problem is that typical American comfort foods are often loaded with unhealthy fats and sugars. Eating high-calorie comfort foods temporarily makes you feel good but, when done in excess, results in an impaired body-mind.

Be mindful of the types of foods you eat by remembering that everything is a form of energy. View food through the lens of energy. This helps you recognize when you are consuming unhealthy energy. Then mindfully make a better choice. Most of us know which foods are healthy and which ones are not. Use mindful eating to help you discern the difference. It's difficult to practice mindful eating when you are starving or feeling hypoglycemic, so eat on a regular schedule to avoid that.

Be mindful of the foods that you eat, and be mindful while you are eating. Entering a state of gratitude before eating supports digestion. This helps calm your autonomic nervous system and increase your parasympathetic nervous system activity. Increasing parasympathetic nervous system activity supports the digestion and absorption of nutrients. Savor each bite, and chew your food mindfully to optimize its digestion and absorption. This is especially important if you have gastrointestinal problems.

Everyday Mindfulness

Use everyday activities to practice fully engaging the present moment. This includes washing the dishes, doing the laundry, weeding your yard, or anything else you regularly do. For example, engage all your senses when washing dishes. Smell the soap and feel the slipperiness of the soap on the dishes. Stay engaged by being aware when your mind wanders. Then bring your attention back to the task at hand. It's easy to get lost in your thoughts when you wash the dishes. When you catch your mind wandering, bring your mind back to the sensations associated with washing dishes. With practice, you get good at mindfully engaging everyday tasks. This simple practice has positive health benefits.

Importance of Mindfulness

Why is mindfulness so important? When you engage the present moment without judgment, you leave behind regrets from your past and worries about your future. When you do this without judgment, your present-moment awareness is free of resistance to what is.

When free of resistance, it's impossible to trigger a stress response. Then your body's autopilot, or autonomic nervous system, begins to balance. Mindfulness and meditation are better than any drug for relaxing and improving your health.

Power of the Present Moment

Everything happens in the present moment. Think about it. Nothing in your life ever takes place in the past or in the future. Everything you do always happens in the present moment. This is why the present moment holds a majority of the powers of action, manifestation, and creation. By practicing mindfulness and meditation, you hone your skill of maximizing present-moment awareness. This maximizes the potential for creating anything you desire in your life.

Types of Meditation

Open awareness meditation involves being fully present without judgment and with no specific awareness. This entails being still and quiet while letting whatever thoughts come into your mind pass without judgment. When you let thoughts arise without judgment, they pass without triggering a stress response. It's like watching balloons fly by without trying to figure out why they are there or where they came from. Just watch, witness, and allow.

Concentration meditation involves focusing on your breath or a mantra. A mantra can be any word or phrase that you say to yourself over and over. You should choose a mantra that is either neutral or calming to you. You'll intuitively know what that is. This lets you peacefully narrow your focus on one specific thing. This prevents distracting thoughts or multitasking in your mind. If your mind starts to wander, come back to your breath or to the repetitive word or phrase.

Mindfulness meditation is a mixture of open awareness and concentration. I just discussed ways to practice mindfulness on a task at hand. Take this practice to the next level by being mindful of something while in a comfortable position with your eyes closed. This can take the form of contemplation or a relaxed focus.

When doing a mindfulness meditation, use diaphragmatic breathing to trigger your relaxation response. This lets your brainwaves slow from a beta predominance to an alpha or theta predominance. This shift reflects a change from excessive thinking to relaxation. When you relax and enter a predominance of alpha or theta brainwaves, you can peacefully contemplate a process or question. This peaceful contemplation can help you release a limiting belief. It can also help you answer a perplexing question. I discuss brainwave states and how to release limiting beliefs in more detail in chapter 7.

Guided visualization meditation involves following someone's voice while letting imagery arise in your mind. This type of meditation lets you get good at visualizing imagery in your mind while maintaining a narrowed focus of thought. Guided imagery is scientifically proven to enhance the immune system. (4)

Heart-centered meditations are powerful meditations because they hold the consciousness of unconditional love. These types of meditations involve conjuring high-energy emotions like love, compassion, and empathy. They also usually involve focusing on your heart area. Science shows these types of meditations balance your autonomic nervous system. (5)

Meditation as a Therapeutic Tool

A 2014 study reviewed forty-seven clinical trials on the effectiveness of meditation. Researchers concluded that meditation programs result in moderate improvement in anxiety, depression, and pain. (6) This study put the traditional medical model's stamp of approval on meditation as a therapeutic tool.

Epigenetics - Turning Genes On and Off

Epigenetics is the study of how your environment turns your genes on and off. It shows that you aren't always at the mercy of your genes. Being born with the genetic predisposition for a disease doesn't necessarily mean you are going to get it.

Genes are the blueprint for your body-mind. Turning them on and off creates wellness or disease. Your environment, including foods, toxins, and thoughts, triggers your genes to turn on and off.

Mind-Body Genomics

Mind-body genomics is the study of how your mind influences your genes to turn on and off. This field of study is in its infancy, but early research is producing some amazing results. By practicing mindfulness and meditation, you learn to regulate your thoughts. By regulating your thoughts, you can trigger your relaxation response. The relaxation response causes genes to turn on and off that optimize your health. A study coauthored by Dr. Herbert Benson in 2013 shows how this happens. (7)

Dr. Benson is a medical doctor and one of the founding fathers of mind-body medicine. He coined the term "relaxation response" almost forty years ago. He says the relaxation response is the opposite of the stress response, and is induced by any mind-body practice that produces relaxation. Dr. Benson set out to study if the relaxation response turned genes on and off. Participants in this study included inexperienced and experienced practitioners of the relaxation response.

Both groups completed eight weekly training sessions. In these training sessions, they learned a relaxation technique, diaphragmatic breathing, body scanning, mantra repetition, and mindfulness meditation. They also listened to a twenty-minute audio track guiding them through the same sequence at home once a day. Researchers analyzed gene expression in participants at the beginning and at the end of the study and here is what they found.

The relaxation response turns on genes involved in the production of energy by mitochondria, which are the batteries of the cell. The relaxation response suppresses inflammation and turns on genes that dampen oxidative stress. This is analogous to reducing body rust. The relaxation response turns on genes increasing insulin production, which has the potential to result in better blood sugar regulation. The relaxation response also has an anti-aging effect, in that it preserves the ends of your chromosomes called telomeres. Not surprisingly, all these beneficial effects were more pronounced in the experienced practitioners.

Meditation Is Anti-inflammatory

Science shows that mindfulness and meditation turn genes on and off to reduce inflammation. Because excessive inflammation causes disease, a reduction in excessive inflammation translates into health benefits. A study published in 2014 shows that the anti-inflammatory effect of mindfulness happens quite rapidly. (8) In this study, a group of expert meditators underwent eight hours of intensive mindfulness.

Researchers performed a gene analysis comparing the expert meditators to a control group who underwent eight hours of quiet nonmeditative activities. What they found was that an intensive day of mindfulness in expert meditators is a powerful anti-inflammatory. It triggered the same gene pathway as the anti-inflammatory drug Celebrex, but without the side effects.

The body creates inflammation through several genetic pathways. One involves a cell protein called nuclear factor kappa B (NFKB). Multiple studies show that mindfulness meditation reduces inflammation by turning off NFKB. (9, 10, 11, 12)

By using mindfulness and meditation to reduce stressful thoughts, you trigger a relaxation response. This relaxation response has a positive influence on how your genes turn on and off, or how they express. So by learning to manipulate your thoughts, you indirectly affect how your genes express. It turns out you can also manipulate your thoughts to grow new neuronal pathways in your brain. Some call this self-directed neuroplasticity.

Self-Directed Neuroplasticity

Neuroplasticity is your brain's ability to physically change and adapt. We used to think that neuroplasticity only occurred in early childhood. We now know that the adult brain is capable of creating new neuronal pathways. Your environment and your actions influence your brain's ability to create new neuronal pathways. This requires a sustained change in your pattern of neural activity. For your brain to create new neuronal pathways, you need to do something in a repetitive manner to create long-lasting changes.

An example of neuroplasticity is what occurs when someone undergoes rehabilitation after a stroke. Rehabilitation to recover neurologic function forces the brain to create new neuronal pathways. These new pathways take over function for the areas of the brain injured by the stroke.

Self-directed neuroplasticity is the ability to create new neuronal connections in your brain through regular mindfulness and meditation. Here's an example. In 2005, researchers imaged the brains of experienced meditators. They found that long-term meditation produces neuroplastic effects. It thickens areas of the brain associated with attention, interoception, and sensory processing. (13) Interoception is your awareness of your body's internal regulation.

These findings were more pronounced in older long-term meditators. It suggests that meditation may help prevent age-related brain atrophy, a common condition in the elderly. A more recent study published in 2015 reinforced this finding. It showed less age-related brain atrophy in long-term meditators compared to those who don't meditate. (14)

Regular meditation is a form of self-directed neuroplasticity. You can use your mind to make positive long-lasting changes in the neuronal pathways of your brain. When you meditate on a regular basis, you get better at holding your attention in the present moment. This may translate into improved focus and less stress. You get better at processing sensory information. This may translate into you becoming more intuitive. You also become more self-aware. This may translate into better self-regulation of your autonomic nervous system. Regular meditation may even help prevent age-related brain atrophy, which has the potential to protect against memory loss and improve brain function as you age.

Imagination Produces Neuroplasticity

Self-directed neuroplasticity also occurs through the process of imagination. In a study published in 1995, participants learned a five-finger piano exercise. One group practiced two hours a day for five days only in their minds. Another group practiced two hours a day on the piano. The results were that five days of mental practice led to the same level of playing skill as three days of actual practice. Participants used imagination to create new neuronal pathways that let them play with the same skill as someone who had practiced on a piano. (15)

By imagining something in your mind, you physically change your brain as long as you imagine it enough. Imagination as a form of self-directed neuroplasticity also helps you develop new skills.

A study published in 2004 shows you can strengthen your muscles by mental training alone. (16) Researchers measured the muscle strength of all participants at the beginning and end of the study. One group of participants mentally performed little finger abduction contractions. A second group mentally performed elbow flexion contractions. A third group acted as a control. The control group did not perform any mental muscle contractions but participated in all measurements.

Mental muscle training lasted fifteen minutes five days per week for twelve weeks. Researchers found that the first group increased finger abduction strength by 35%. The second group increased elbow flexion strength by 13.5%. The control group showed no significant increases in strength. Mental training is effective because it changes the brain, resulting in increased muscle strength.

Athletes know that visualizing a movement or routine improves their ability to perform it. (17) Visualization does more than just help them memorize a routine. It strengthens muscles and improves coordination as if they were performing the technique.

Science suggests that imagination in the form of visualization has a vast untapped potential. Your imagination is way more powerful than you think, so use it wisely.

Overcoming Your Resistance to Meditation

When you first start meditating, your body-mind may pull you back into old and familiar patterns. Even if your behavior causes suffering, your mind will hold on to it out of familiarity. The mind thinks, "I know this causes me to suffer, but at least I know what I'm in for." At first there may be a little breaking-in period where you have to push through a discomfort zone of change. That's okay. Keep pushing because the rewards are huge and the discomfort zone won't last long.

Your mind may also project fears and negativity into the present moment as a form of distraction. You might hear thoughts in your mind like "This is not going to work for me," or "I'm wasting my time with this stuff." Use mindfulness to acknowledge any fears or negativity, but know this isn't the truth. Doing this causes the negative thoughts and fears to subside.

When you begin practicing mindfulness and meditation, consider doing it with a partner. You and your partner can encourage and motivate each other. This is like having a workout partner, though you don't have to meditate together. Just make regular calls or send reminders to each other. Also, share information about your experiences to help keep each other on track.

Set electronic reminders for mindfulness and meditation on your smartphone or computer. You should also place post-it notes around your home and office as a reminder. By making these reminders in the form of positive affirmations, you reinforce positive thinking and balance out any negative thinking that may arise.

In chapter 8, I provide a list of core positive affirmations. I also show you the effective way to use positive affirmations. It's important to know how to use positive affirmations effectively. This is because they don't work well unless you create the right conditions for their use.

Finally, I recommend you keep a journal when you start practicing mindfulness and meditation. Journaling is a great way to track your progress. It also allows you to document epiphanies and breakthroughs, which you will experience.

I hope the evidence I've presented incentivizes you to practice mindfulness and meditation. Consistent practice creates deep neuronal pathways of peace in your brain. It also helps you develop and master powerful new skills.

Chapter 3
Stress

STRESS COMES IN MANY FORMS, including emotional and physical stressors. Stress and its sources are forms of energy, because everything is made up of energy. It's a universal law.

Physical stressors include structural abnormalities, metabolic dysfunction, chronic infection, and toxins. Emotional stress is a negative emotional response to the way you perceive your environment. Emotional stress also comes in the form of unresolved old emotional conflicts. This includes a lack of forgiveness and longstanding anger, fear, and rage about past experiences. Unresolved emotional conflicts may be conscious or unconscious.

Unresolved Emotional Conflicts

Unresolved emotional conflicts often originate in childhood. These emotional conflicts contribute to self-loathing and poor self-esteem. This is especially common in sensitive children who have experienced emotional and physical abuse or trauma.

I've seen many patients who thought they had let go of an old emotional conflict only to see it arise after deep introspection. If a memory creates a negative charge or sensation in your body-mind, this means an associated emotional conflict is unresolved. A negative charge can manifest as tension or tightness in the body, or as emotional or physical pain. You have a choice to strengthen this internal conflict by giving it energy. Thought creates this energy by ruminating on the perceived slight, which drives the negative emotions associated with it. Or you can choose to work through the unresolved emotional conflict and let it go.

Working through an unresolved emotional conflict and letting it go requires several important components. First, you must be ready to see the original event that created the conflict. Second, you must see this original event with a peaceful higher awareness. As I've discussed before, you can use meditation to achieve this higher awareness.

I've created a meditation technique to let you do this. By seeing the original event with a higher emotional intelligence, it no longer triggers a stress response. You also gain a sense of empowerment. This is important because unresolved emotional conflicts usually involve feeling disempowered.

By seeing it through the eyes of a safe and empowered you, you'll gain new insights. You'll view the original event with a new perspective that rewrites the original experience. When this happens, the original event no longer hijacks your primitive nervous system to create a stress response. It was this primitive stress response that helped create this unresolved emotional conflict. This is one of many ways to tap into the vast healing powers of the mind.

You may hold on to an old, unresolved emotional conflict because you feel it empowers you in some way. Someone may believe that holding on to anger empowers him or her by serving as a reminder to never let a similar situation happen again. This is how you might try to rationalize a mindset that contains an illusion of safety. In reality, holding on to anger actually serves as a reminder of feeling unsafe. This keeps your nervous system in a subtle, if not overt, stress response. This perpetual emotional stressor eventually results in a breakdown of your body's systems.

Mindsets that create an illusion of safety while triggering a stress response are clearly unhealthy. Unresolved emotional conflicts may falsely empower your ego. They also disempower the longstanding health of your body-mind. Unresolved emotional conflicts trigger a negative physiologic reaction in your body-mind. It does this by locking your autonomic nervous system into a chronic stress response. Suppressing old emotional conflicts lets negative energy smolder in your subconscious mind. At some point, these embers may create a catastrophic fire.

Your subconscious mind is like a hard drive on a computer and has the potential to remember every event in your life. If one of these memories contains an unresolved emotional conflict, it acts like a virus affecting your entire body-mind. There are ways to search your subconscious hard drive for these viruses and delete them. I'll describe one such technique later in the book.

The Stress Response

The stress response is a psychobiological phenomenon. It starts in the mind and then negatively impacts the body. We all experience stress, and sometimes a little stress is good for you. The problem is that when stress is mismanaged over prolonged periods, it has a detrimental effect on your body-mind.

Some estimate that 60% to 90% of all doctor visits are stress related. That estimate is likely accurate, because we are a body-mind, not a separate body and mind. Prolonged mismanaged stress worsens any acute or chronic health condition. Mismanaged stress can also help trigger any underlying diseases you may be genetically at risk for.

Stress as an Epigenetic Influencer

Remember when I said you're not always at the mercy of your genes. You may be born with a genetic risk for a disease, but you aren't always going to develop it. Your environment, including toxic thoughts, turns genes on and off to create disease. The relaxation response reduces excessive inflammation in the body by turning on and off certain genes. Chronic, uncontrolled stress creates excessive inflammation that causes diseases. When chronically stressed, it's unlikely you'll be experiencing much of a relaxation response.

Emotional Stress Starts with Perception

People give various reasons for emotional stress. They'll cite finances, children, school, or work. What they usually leave out of the equation is that emotional stress always starts with their perception. Here's an example. You and I have a neighbor who likes to prank people. We both live across the street from him. I think his antics are hilarious, and you think his actions are dreadful. I'm waiting for the next prank, and you want him removed from the neighborhood. What is the difference between you and me? The answer is perception.

Countering Stress with Nonresistance

The most important point about perception causing stress is that it's always caused by resistance to what is. When you feel resistance about something, it triggers a stress response. If you aren't resisting something, it's not going to trigger a stress response. You can use mindfulness and meditation to learn how to enter a state of nonresistance.

Nonresistance doesn't mean letting someone or a situation take advantage of you. It's about using mindfulness to go into a place of nonresistance about it. When you do this, you experience peacefulness. Peacefulness attained through mindfulness and meditation is associated with a higher awareness. This higher awareness gives you clarity about appropriate actions to take.

Creating periods of nonresistance is about creating balance in your life. Sometimes you need to be highly reactive very quickly to avoid a dangerous situation. Sometimes a little drama results in you making important changes in your life. This is about practicing the art of nonresistance through mindfulness and meditation and then incorporating periods of nonresistance to balance excessive stress responses.

You might meditate on the experience with your neighbor with a goal of being less reactive. Another goal would be to meditate on why he triggers such a visceral reaction in you. You might find that he reminds you of someone who bullied you in the past. Or he reminds you of an ex-spouse. With this awareness, you can view the situation with a higher emotional intelligence. This lets you respond in a healthier way rather than react with rage. This higher awareness can defuse your rage and let you perceive the situation differently. It's worth a try if it will help you remedy the problem without creating an excessive stress response. Armed with this higher awareness, you might then have a peaceful discussion with your neighbor, asking him to tone down the pranks. Using emotional intelligence to communicate with people through a higher awareness is quite effective.

Your beliefs, along with your experiences, help to create your perception. Regular mindfulness and meditation lets you cultivate a higher awareness about yourself and your life. When you bring in this higher awareness, you begin to bring choice to your perception. This means you can choose a different perception about your experience. This reduces your overall stress response. It may take a regular practice of mindfulness and meditation to train your mind to cultivate this higher awareness.

Stress Causes an Imbalanced Autonomic Nervous System

When you mismanage stress for long periods, your autonomic nervous system gets imbalanced. Your autonomic nervous system consists of two main parts — sympathetic and parasympathetic. Your sympathetic nervous system regulates your fight-or-flight stress response. Your parasympathetic nervous system regulates your rest-and-digest relaxation response.

Long-term stress generally creates an imbalance of high sympathetic activity and low parasympathetic activity. The resulting predominant chronic fight-or-flight response causes a breakdown of your body's systems. Our bodies can handle transient stress, but when stress becomes chronic, disease ensues.

Chronically Mismanaged Stress Causes Memory Loss

A chronic stress response wreaks havoc on a part of your brain called the hippocampus. Your hippocampus is loaded with glucocorticoid receptors. These receptors interact with hormones triggered by the stress response. When overstimulated, the hippocampus starts to poop out, resulting in hippocampal degeneration. Degeneration of the hippocampus causes memory loss. This is why many chronically stressed people have trouble with their memory.

Chronically Mismanaged Stress Causes
Hormone Imbalances

Chronic unregulated stress also results in an imbalance in your hypothalamic-pituitary-thyroid-adrenal-gonadal (HPTAG) axis. This axis is your hormone system that begins in your hypothalamus. This is followed by your pituitary gland, thyroid gland, adrenal glands, and your gonads, whether testes or ovaries. Chronic mismanaged stress is one reason why so many people have hormone problems. Examples include early menopause in women and low testosterone in men.

The adrenal glands weaken under chronic stress because they are the main endocrine regulator of the stress response. When weakened, the adrenals go into a state of dysregulation. Disrupted hormone output from the adrenals skews the entire HPTAG axis. When this happens, the body starts to prioritize what it can repair versus what it's just going to let go. It's no wonder that the gonads — testicles and ovaries — start to lose their function. The body says, "Okay, I'm going to let the gonads go, because I can survive without them. I can't survive without the adrenals and the pituitary."

This is an overly simplistic view, but you get the idea. There are other contributors to hormonal problems like obesity and endocrine disruptors in chemicals. But chronically mismanaged stress is a major player.

People with mismanaged stress may experience adrenal fatigue syndrome. This is a controversial topic, as the traditional medical model says the condition doesn't exist. Functional medicine teaches otherwise. As far as adrenal dysfunction, traditional medicine says you either have Cushing's syndrome or Addison's disease.

Cushing's syndrome is an overproduction of cortisol. Addison's disease is full-blown adrenal failure. In reality, your body is a dynamic organism with various stages of function. There are no peer-reviewed clinical studies proving the existence of adrenal fatigue syndrome. Despite that, functional medicine practitioners opt to treat this condition with variable success. Whether the measures these practitioners take directly addresses adrenal fatigue syndrome or shores up the rest of the body to repair stress induced damage remains to be elucidated in clinical trials. I suspect the answer is both.

Adrenal fatigue syndrome takes into account various stages of adrenal dysregulation. It may play a role in chronic health issues such as impaired immunity, chronic fatigue syndrome, and fibromyalgia. Prolonged adrenal fatigue syndrome causes you to lose the ability to regulate inflammation. Some inflammation is important for survival. Proper function of your immune system requires an appropriate inflammatory response. But when chronic inflammation goes unchecked, health problems arise. Studies show that uncontrolled inflammation is a root cause of the vast majority of chronic illnesses. (18, 19, 20, 21, 22)

When multiple body systems become dysfunctional, people get really sick. Now you see why chronically mismanaged stress results in disease. So how do we counter the stress response? The answer lies in creating balance.

To help manage stress, first use mindfulness and meditation to develop a higher awareness. This higher awareness gives you choices of perception. Becoming aware of these choices lets you change perceptions about your experiences. Changing perception helps you to avoid a hopeless scenario in your mind.

When you practice mindfulness and meditation, you learn how to trigger your relaxation response. Relaxation positively impacts your body-mind. It even turns genes turn on and off to improve your health.

Chapter 4
Functional Medicine Guidelines

FUNCTIONAL MEDICINE IS A SYSTEMS-ORIENTED approach to medical care. It addresses the whole person and not just an isolated set of symptoms. This approach also engages patients as a therapeutic partner and supports the unique expression of health and vitality for each individual. In this chapter, I discuss general functional medicine guidelines to optimize your health.

Optimize Nutrition

Optimal nutrition is key for good health. Phytonutrients in food communicate with your genes by turning genes on and off. For example, nutrient-rich whole foods trigger anti-inflammatory genes. Processed foods high in sugar and unhealthy fats trigger genes to produce excessive inflammation.

Human life originated in an intelligent ecosystem designed for us to thrive. Take advantage of this natural ecosystem by eating a predominantly plant-based whole food diet. Make organic fruits and vegetables a regular staple in your diet to avoid exposure to pesticides and other toxins. Colorful fruits and vegetables and spices are loaded with phytonutrients and fiber. They optimize how your genes express and are natural anti-inflammatories. The best fruits to eat are blueberries, blackberries, and raspberries because they are relatively low in sugar compared to other types of fruits. Berries are also rich in healthy phytonutrients. A predominantly plant-based diet loaded with fiber helps with proper regulation of blood sugar. Avoid unnatural processed foods.

Avoid or reduce potatoes, rice, and other grains because they are high-glycemic-index foods, which rapidly turn to sugar in the body and interfere with proper blood sugar metabolism. Foods that are high in sugar or rapidly turn to sugar in the body also let potentially pathogenic bacteria and yeast thrive in your gastrointestinal tract and help create an unhealthy ratio of good to bad microorganisms in your gut.

Eat high-quality proteins, including organic grass-fed meats, wild game, and wild-caught fish. Typical meats in the standard American diet (SAD) contain antibiotics, hormones, and pesticides due to how the animals are fed and raised. Optimal meats come from animals that are wild or pastured, allowed to free range, and eat grass and insects. Conventionally raised animals are fed pesticide-laden grains that make their meat higher in inflammatory omega-6 fatty acids.

Farm-raised fish are also fed grains, which changes their meat from a healthy omega-3 fatty acid predominance into an unhealthy omega-6 fatty acid predominance. When consumed, omega-6 fatty acids are inflammatory whereas omega-3 fatty acids are anti-inflammatory. In addition, farm-raised fish are more likely to contain chemicals, antibiotics, and pesticides. When choosing wild-caught fish, choose smaller fish such as salmon, mackerel, and sardines as they are less likely to contain mercury than larger predator fish such as swordfish, tuna, and sea bass.

Eat plenty of raw nuts and seeds. Avoid commercially dry-roasted nuts and seeds as the way they are processed makes it more likely the oils they contain will be oxidized or rancid. It's optimal to soak raw nuts and seeds for about twenty-four hours before consuming so as to optimize their digestion.

Finally, consume plenty of healthy fats such as cold-pressed extra virgin olive oil, avocado oil, and flax oil. Cook with extra virgin coconut oil and ghee.

Nutritional Supplements

Not everyone needs nutritional supplementation. If you are chronically ill or chronically stressed, you may benefit from nutritional supplementation. Always try to get your vitamins and minerals from a nutrient dense diet. If you don't consistently eat a healthy diet, consider a high-quality multivitamin-multimineral supplement.

Consider taking a multivitamin-multimineral containing methylated folic acid and methylated vitamin B12. Methylated folic acid and vitamin B12 are biologically active forms of these vitamins. Examples of methylated folic acid are methylfolate and methylenetetrahydrofolate. Methylated B12 includes methylcobalamin and hydroxocobalamin.

Nutrition Affects Gene Expression and Genes Affect Nutrition Needs

Nutrigenomics is the study of how nutrition status affects gene expression and how genes affect nutrition needs. For example, some individuals don't produce adequate amounts of an enzyme called methylenetetrahydrofolate reductase (MTHFR) because of their unique genes. MTHFR is a key enzyme in a biochemical process called methylation. Methylation is important for cellular repair, detoxification, neurotransmitter production, and proper immune function. Both folic acid and vitamin B12 are critical factors in this methylation process.

Four bases — adenine, guanine, cytosine, and thymine — make up each segment of DNA. The sequence of these four bases determines the genetic information carried in each segment. Single nucleotide polymorphisms (SNPs) are variations in the sequence of these four bases. When SNPs occur, they produce variants of that gene. SNPs that occur in the gene that produces MTHFR result in an enzyme with decreased activity.

If this SNP is heterozygous with one affected gene and one normal gene, the MTHFR enzyme functions at about 60%. If this mutation is homozygous with both genes affected, the MTHFR enzyme functions at about 10–30%.

MTHFR deficiency is a common genetic mutation. It also limits the conversion of folic acid to its biologically active form.

Variants of MTHFR deficiency are associated with chronic diseases such as attention deficit hyperactivity disorder, cancer, cardiovascular disease, and depression.

Using nutritional supplements to address MTHFR deficiency is controversial. This is because the science is still evolving. Some individuals with an MTHFR deficiency may require methylated folic acid to improve their health. Supplementing with folic acid can mask a B12 deficiency, so it's a good idea to also supplement with methylated B12.

Some individuals with MTHFR deficiency may experience side effects when taking methylated folic acid. This is due to the coexistence of other types of SNPs that interfere with proper metabolism. If you decide to supplement with methylated folic acid, start out low (400 mcg) and slow (every other day). If you experience worsening of any symptoms, stop the supplement.

Functional medicine practitioners receive training in nutrition and the proper use of nutritional supplementation. I recommend consulting with a licensed functional medicine practitioner when using nutritional supplements. This is especially true when dealing with nutritional issues related to SNPs.

MTHFR DNA mutation analysis is a blood test available through labs like LabCorp and Quest Diagnostics. This test tells you if you have an MTHFR deficiency. It should only be ordered and interpreted by a licensed healthcare practitioner. This test is something to consider if you have chronic unexplained symptoms or a chronic health condition that's not improving or is getting worse.

Sunlight and Vitamin D

Vitamin D deficiency is an epidemic. This is because we live indoors, mostly work indoors, and many people get little sunlight. Some people have become afraid of sunlight. Sunlight is a very important part of our natural ecosystem and is essential for optimal health. Sun exposure should not be demonized but considered with common sense. A recent study found that avoidance of sun exposure is a risk factor for death of a similar magnitude as smoking. (23)

Sunlight is necessary for adequate production of vitamin D. If you don't get regular sun exposure, get your vitamin D level tested. Then adjust your sun exposure or supplement with vitamin D based on the results. Your healthcare practitioner should guide you on this matter.

Beneficial Bacteria

Beneficial bacteria in your intestines are essential for optimal health. This is because they help you digest food and maintain a healthy immune system. Eat fermented foods or take a probiotic to maintain adequate levels of beneficial gut bacteria. It is preferable to eat fermented foods like organic yogurt, kefir, kimchi, or sauerkraut on a regular basis. This is a natural way to help maintain beneficial bacteria in your gastrointestinal tract.

A healthy gut is important for your overall health because the gut associated lymphoid tissue (GALT) lines your gastrointestinal tract. This GALT makes up the vast majority of your immune system. An imbalance of good to bad gut microbes may result in dysfunction of your entire immune system.

Overgrowth of yeast, parasites, and potentially pathogenic bacteria in the gut is common. This is especially true in people with chronic health problems. Functional medicine practitioners look upstream for root causes of chronic health conditions. They order innovative tests to determine if there is a gut microbial imbalance. To find a functional medicine practitioner, go to www.functionalmedicine.org. On the home page, click on the tab that lets you search for a practitioner in your area.

Consider taking a broad-spectrum probiotic to improve your health. Studies show certain beneficial bacteria can improve certain health conditions. But these studies can't possibly account for all the health variables in every individual. This is another reason why it's a good idea to enlist the aid of a functional medicine practitioner to guide your probiotic choices.

Magnesium

Some people may benefit from taking magnesium. Magnesium deficiency is the most common mineral deficiency. Magnesium is a relaxant and may help alleviate chronic muscle tension, cramps, insomnia, and constipation. Get magnesium in your diet by eating leafy greens, nuts, and seeds. Be careful not to take too much supplemental magnesium because it can act as a laxative.

When taking magnesium, start with small doses. A powder form may be easier to adjust the dose than pills. Stay away from magnesium oxide unless you are severely constipated. This is because the magnesium oxide is more stimulating to the gut. Consider other types of chelated magnesium like magnesium citrate or magnesium aspartate. And don't supplement with magnesium if you have any form of kidney dysfunction.

Always discuss nutritional supplementation with a qualified healthcare practitioner before beginning any regimen. Traditionally trained doctors are not adequately educated in nutrition. Most functional medicine practitioners are quite capable of guiding you on proper supplement recommendations.

Avoidance of Toxins

Avoiding toxins is another way to strengthen your body's foundational support. Do your best to avoid environmental toxins, because they literally poison your body. How well you are able to detoxify specific toxins depends on your genes and your overall body burden of toxins. You can't change the genes you were born with, but you can avoid toxins.

Choose more natural cleaners and cosmetics. Avoid spraying chemical pesticides in and around your home. I choose an all-natural pest control service, which works as well as any other pest control I've ever used. This natural pest control uses substances like diatomaceous earth and essential oils. It's up to you to seek out these types of alternative products and services from established companies with a good track record. An excellent website for education and resources about avoiding environmental toxins is www.ewg.org.

Exercise

It's important that you get moving. Exercise is one of the most studied and proven natural therapies for maintaining and improving your health. Lack of exercise contributes to escalating rates of type 2 diabetes and other obesity-related diseases. The elderly can benefit from regular walking or other programs like chair yoga. Regular exercise helps you sleep better, but exercising late in the evening may interfere with falling asleep.

Get Out in Nature

Get out in nature for adequate sun exposure and fresh air. Vitamin D deficiency is an epidemic and contributes to more chronic diseases than just osteoporosis. (24)

Unless you are on medications or have a disease like discoid lupus that make you sensitive to sunlight, get adequate amounts of sunlight without overdoing it. Get out in nature, breathe fresh air, and interact with the energies of nature. Science shows that grounding yourself to the earth (earthing), like I described in the grounding visualization, acts as a natural anti-inflammatory. (25)

Get Adequate Sleep

Adequate sleep should be a major priority, because the bulk of your body's repair processes take place during sleep. Sleep requirements vary depending on the individual. Aim for seven to eight hours of sleep each night. Some people need more, depending on their lifestyles and health issues.

Sleep is when your body does most of its repair, rebalancing, rejuvenation, and recovery. Your brain also processes memory and daily events while you are sleeping. A study on mice in 2013 showed that the brain detoxifies waste products during sleep. (26)

Besides avoiding stimulants like caffeine in the afternoon, some people may benefit from removing electronics from the bedroom. This is because some people are sensitive to electromagnetic fields. (27) Electronic equipment in the bedroom can potentially interfere with sleep. So if you have trouble sleeping, remove electronics from your bedroom and see if you sleep better. If you use your smartphone as an alarm clock, put it in airplane mode before falling asleep. Cell phones emit strong electromagnetic fields and can negatively impact those who are sensitive to electromagnetic fields.

Avoid reading electronic devices in bed. The type of light emitted by these devices may interfere with the release of melatonin by your pineal gland. (28) Melatonin helps initiate sleep. Artificial light entering your eyes at bedtime overrides the natural release of melatonin associated with darkness.

Try to sleep in complete darkness to stimulate the natural release of melatonin. If you have insomnia, consider avoiding alcohol. In many individuals, alcohol interferes with adequate stages of sleep, specifically REM sleep. (29)

Some people find that taking a warm bath in the evening helps their muscles relax. Adding Epsom salt or sea salt to your bath water may help you relax because magnesium in these salts is absorbed through the skin and acts as a relaxant.

These functional medicine concepts are some simple but effective ways to help optimize your health. I recommend that you enlist the help of a healthcare practitioner trained in functional medicine if you'd like to explore them further.

Chapter 5
Everything Is Energy

EVERYTHING IN OUR UNIVERSE, INCLUDING your body-mind, is made up of energy. Science says our universe began as a massive release of energy known as the Big Bang. Shortly after the Big Bang, temperatures started to cool and mass began to form. Einstein's equation $E = mc^2$ alludes to the fact that mass and energy are interchangeable. We are in the form of a body but made up of energy.

Clues that we are energetic beings are shown by the ability to electrically measure body function. An electrocardiogram (ECG) measures the electrical activity of the heart. An electroencephalogram (EEG) measures the electrical activity of the brain. And an electromyogram (EMG) measures the electrical activity of muscles.

Energy relates to mindfulness and meditation in that consciousness as thoughts is made up of energy. Intercessory prayer is an effective player in healing because you transmit energy when you pray. (30, 31, 32)

Let's dig a little deeper into how you can manipulate energy to positively impact your body-mind. Keep in mind that some of the concepts I present about energy are theoretical. This is because science is still exploring the energetic universe.

Scientists are attempting to define all the energy particles at the subatomic level. This quest is what helps fund projects like the Large Hadron Collider in Europe. The Large Hadron Collider is a massive machine that collides particles of energy and analyzes the results. Scientists hope to devise a mathematical model that explains how all the energies in our universe interact — a unified field theory. The unified field connects the energies of everyone and everything, including the consciousness of the divine.

It is in this yet undiscovered mathematical model of the unified field theory where science and spirituality merge. By aligning the energy of your consciousness with the divine energy of the unified field, you access the paranormal, the miraculous, and the spiritual. Intuitively, we know this unified field exists, and scientists are spending billions of dollars to prove it. A better understanding of energy will bridge the gap between science and spirituality and ultimately explain this unified field.

Everything is energy, including your consciousness as thoughts, intentions, and prayers. Because consciousness is energetic, it impacts your body in powerful ways that can't always be predicted. This is why it's important to consider the energetic aspect of everything.

For example, consider the energetic aspect of food. Does the food you eat contain good energy? Nutrient dense natural foods contain higher energy than processed foods full of chemicals and preservatives.

Consider the energetic aspect of relationships. Optimal relationships offer an equal exchange of energy. This isn't always possible when taking care of someone like a child or a sick person. An unequal exchange of energy in relationships over prolonged periods depletes the energy of the person providing the most energy. If a relationship involves taking care of another person, regularly recharge yourself through self-care. Self-care includes mindfulness, meditation, yoga, prayer, exercise, adequate rest, and massage. If possible, find a way to share care-taking responsibilities.

Viewing life through an energetic lens may make it easier to decide about making changes to improve your life. Healthy relationships with good boundaries require mindfulness and high emotional intelligence. Mindfulness and meditation increase emotional intelligence by giving you a higher awareness about yourself, your situations, and your relationships.

Quantum Physics

How might all this relate to quantum physics? Quantum physics is about energetic relationships at an atomic and subatomic level. Here energy behaves almost magically, existing as both a wave and a particle depending on the observer. At the quantum level, energy behaves differently than at the macroscopic level of our lives. It's easier to see a direct relationship between cause and effect at the macroscopic level than at the subatomic level.

By macroscopic, I mean the level at which we are objectively interacting with our environment.

In quantum physics, energy exists in two forms — a wave and a particle. The catch is that these two forms exist in a realm of probabilities and the observer decides which. The double slit experiment proves this. But physicists say the observer is the mechanical device that detects the energy, and not the human observer.

Some people attempt to equate this concept with the ability of humans to simply intend an outcome. Most physicists say the rules at the quantum level do not apply at the macroscopic level, and that saying otherwise is magical thinking. There is a lot of talk about setting your intention, and you as the observer being able to decide if something manifests in your life.

Setting an intention does help you manifest something, but manifesting at the macroscopic level always requires action. The problem is that science hasn't yet figured out all the energetic components of intention and action. It's not simple because so many complex variables are involved in manifestation. But you can learn to maximize the energies of intention through mindfulness and meditation to help create what you want.

You can use the analogy of the quantum observer to play with the idea of manifesting at the macroscopic level through thought and intention. Just don't get overly caught up in the idea that you can manifest by just wishing it so.

There are examples of magical manifesting in the Bible and other ancient texts. Those examples involved people who had learned to master the energies of our universe, including the spiritual realm. I would argue that manifesting by intention plays a role in some cases of spontaneous remission of stage IV cancers. This is a controversial topic and all the components of how this occurs have yet to be discovered. Just like all of the energetic components of our universe have yet to be discovered.

The fact that spontaneous remission of stage IV cancers and other terminal diseases does happen points to the seemingly magical abilities of our body-mind. By magical, I mean abilities not explained by science. Just because these abilities are not explained by science does not mean they don't exist. We just currently don't have the technological ability to explain how.

In the Quantum Connection guided meditation at the end of this chapter, I guide you through becoming aware of empty space. I do this to get you out of your monkey mind and to trigger your relaxation response. I want you to practice visualizing, experiencing, and becoming aware of emptiness. The paradox is that there is no such thing as empty space in our universe, except possibly in black holes. This is because empty space contains some type of energy.

Even though you can't see the individual energetic parts of the rays of our sun, you know it's there because you can feel it. The residual of the sun's energy is there even after the sun dips beyond the horizon. You can feel the residual of the sun's energy after sunset by touching a rock that was lit by the sun.

The sun's energy, like all energy, contains intelligent information. This information tells receptors in the leaves of plants to initiate photosynthesis. It also tells receptors in our skin to initiate the production of vitamin D. Your thoughts also permeate empty space and contain intelligent information.

Another way to think about empty space and energy is how you communicate with someone with a cell phone. As long as you are in the range of a cell phone tower or Wi-Fi, you transfer your voice in the form of energy through empty space into your friend's cell phone. Their cell phone then translates an energetic signal into your voice.

This may be the way energy works from a consciousness perspective. Our thoughts are energies being transmitted into empty space. Those energies merge with other energies. Just because we can't see these energies doesn't mean they don't exist. You can't see the energy that transmits your voice through a cell phone but you know it's there.

Consciousness permeates empty space just like a cell phone's waves of energy. We just don't have the scientific technology to measure the energy of consciousness. This is how intercessory prayer may be effective for some individuals.

Because empty space is full of energy, it's full of potential. This is analogous to using the power of the present moment to create something. The present moment is full of potential. Nothing ever happens in the past or the future. Everything happens in the present moment. By fully engaging the present moment, you tap into a vast reservoir of potential energy to create something.

The Quantum Connection meditation guides you through an analogy of entering empty space teeming with energy to create something new with a clean palette. It is in this empty space containing energy where we can create miracles. The energy of the present moment is teeming with the infinite potential of creation.

When doing the Quantum Connection meditation, visualize entering this empty space as pure energy. When you visualize becoming pure energy, you become pure consciousness. In doing so, you engage the present moment without anchors from your past or worries about your future. The key to ramping up this process is to bring in high-energy feelings of unconditional love and deep trust.

Quantum Connection Technique

I start this guided meditation by having you visualize empty space. This is a technique I first read about in Dr. Les Fehmi's book The Open-Focus Brain. It is a genius concept, as it takes you out of your analytical mind by focusing on something very abstract.

Empty space is teeming with energy, including the energy of consciousness. While contemplating empty space, imagine becoming the energy of consciousness. Combine this practice with your spiritual beliefs by using a higher awareness to merge your energy with the energy of divine consciousness.

You can practice being the quantum observer and creating whatever outcome you wish to achieve. Imagination is a powerful facilitator of creation because it changes your brain through neuroplasticity. Be in and become one with the energy of this empty space. One of the goals is to tap into the energy of divine creation to create whatever it is you want in your life. If you'll notice, what I'm doing is defining the process of prayer though the lens of energy.

Because humans didn't create our species, there has to be some beautiful divine energy that birthed us and facilitates our experiences. If you wish, you can use this meditation to tap into that divine energy. Or not. It's up to you.

Use this technique as a way to acknowledge your power, even if it is simply acknowledging the power of your intention. Start by believing in the power of your intention to help manifest something. If you don't believe in this process, it may be less likely to happen.

Placebo effect research proves that believing in something is powerful. Later in the book, I describe my experience with clairvoyance — an unexplained knowing. It was quite magical. But if I hadn't believed that I could have a clairvoyant type of experience, I might not have ever had that type of experience. Without opening my mind to that potential, I might have shut myself out of that experience by placing myself in a rigid dogmatic box about how life works. But I didn't do that. I opened my mind by believing it was possible and I had that experience.

Know that you can have these types of magical experiences, but you need to bring that possibility into your belief system. By going into the space of pure energy, you can use that place as a starting point for powerful conscious creation.

The Unified Field Is Conscious

I believe our universe is a supremely intelligent and conscious living entity. It contains vast amounts of energetic information in a unified field of energy. What follows is a theoretical explanation of how energies interact in our universe to create what we know and also what we don't know. Some of the content is scientifically proven while other parts are based on my intuition.

This explanation is not meant to be purely scientific, so bring along your curiosity and imagination while I take a stab at explaining the unexplainable. I'm going to warn you. I get a little nerdy in the next section because it contains a fair amount of science, so bear with me.

Energy of Consciousness — the Great Influencer

Energy is the fabric of the universe, and all matter originates from energy. Energy is information including thoughts, prayers, intentions, and beliefs. Regarding this, some of the highest energetic frequencies in consciousness are universal spiritual truths found in all of the sacred texts.

Consciousness is the omniscient information field that connects everyone and everything. The energy field of consciousness includes the following:

- Subconscious and conscious thought forms of all humans
- Consciousness of the soul — higher self
- Consciousness of all that is created by the divine — the universe
- Consciousness of the divine

Concepts in physics are evolving based on new findings in the cosmos, which may require a complete rethinking of Einstein's law of relativity. (33) Not only is the concept of energy shifting on the physical plane of mathematical laws as new discoveries are made in our universe, but a major shift is occurring in global consciousness. Researchers at the Institute of HeartMath say, "Humankind is in the middle of a great paradigm shift from a mentality of competition to one of cooperation." (34)

As the human race goes through the great change of transformation in consciousness to create new systems of cooperation and unity on earth, the energetic push comes from the frequencies encoded in your DNA. These frequencies include lower vibrational shadow frequencies associated with fear and higher vibrational gift frequencies associated with love. (35)

As you transcend your fears and come into a state of unconditional love, you transform your consciousness to a higher frequency band that energizes your DNA, creating profound healing in your body-mind. DNA is a biologic quantum field computer, and as such, connects you to the energies of the spiritual dimension and consciousness. (36)

All energies influence each other, sometimes in subtle, but more often in highly significant and unusual ways. If energy waves come together in coherence forming a constructive interference pattern, they create an energy wave of higher amplitude. This increases the amount of energy carried by the wave. Increasing the energy of a wave has the potential to amplify its effect on matter, including your body-mind.

Quantum coherence, or coherence of energy at a subatomic level, adds the quality of entanglement. Entanglement is the ability of energy particles, such as photons, to communicate even if on opposite sides of the universe. Einstein described this phenomenon as "spooky action at a distance." Entangled energy particles, even when separated by great distances, don't exist in a specific state until measured, but once measured, are able to communicate their state to each other instantaneously. (37) This communication happens faster than the speed of light, which violates Einstein's theory of relativity. (38)

Energy in many forms is constantly influencing your physical body. Epigenetics is the study of how your environment affects gene expression, or how genes are turned on or off. Energetic waveforms predominating in the body are the ones that potentially have the strongest epigenetic influence. Meaning if you are constantly in a state of anger or dissatisfaction, then that prevailing emotion experienced as an energetic thought form may create an overriding epigenetic influence on how your genes are expressed. Gene expression triggered by stressful emotions can be harmful, whereas gene expression triggered by thoughts and practices inducing the relaxation response can be beneficial. (39)

As a quantum intention, every thought has the potential power of prayer. This is because all energy contains information, and as an intention, it also contains consciousness. When an energetic waveform of a specific intention comes into coherence with another waveform, its impact on matter results in conscious creation. Learning how to transmute negative thought forms is a powerful way to positively influence your environment, especially your body-mind.

There are ways to create coherent waveforms in your body that positively influence core parts of you associated with intuition and non-verbal communication. The main regulator of these abilities is your heart's energy field. (40) Regular practice of creating coherent energy fields in the heart through techniques developed by HeartMath, much like practicing to play the guitar or learning how to speak a new language, can be honed. And with regular practice, it becomes second nature.

Fractals — the Great Stabilizer

So what stabilizes all of these energy waves flying through our universe? The answer could be found in fractals, which create an efficient and structured energetic highway upon which to travel. Fractals originate as an alignment of repeating energy vectors that provide for a stable interconnectedness of all energy systems in the universe. Since these fractals are energetic in origin, and since energy influences matter, they leave their mark in matter by creating repeating patterns seen throughout nature. (41) These repeating patterns are also found in the human body, serving as a reminder that we all originated from the same source, and we are all connected.

Fractals display self-similarity. This is reflected by the ability of objects to exhibit the same type of structure in all scales, large or small. Fractals give sacred geometry and snowflakes their structure. You can also find fractal patterns in the branches of a tree, fronds of a plant, crystals, ocean waves, earthquakes, and even DNA. (42) Not surprisingly, since fractals originate as energy vectors, they are also observed in coherence patterns of brain function and in heart rate variability analysis. (43, 44)

Dark energy existing in dark matter consists of energy vectors creating repeating fractals, and is what gives our universe energetic stability through similarity in structure. The energetic influence of fractals is represented mathematically, allowing for the actual measurements of the physical components of these fractals. Mathematical expressions of fractals are seen in the golden ratio, Penrose tiling, and the Fibonacci sequence. The golden ratio is a number found by dividing a line in two parts so that the longer part divided by the smaller part is equal to the whole length divided by the longer part. Roger Penrose, a professor of mathematics and physics, established that a surface could be tiled in an asymmetrical, non-repeating pattern using five-fold symmetry with two shapes based on the golden ratio. This pattern, named Penrose tiling, was later discovered to exist in nature as the structure of quasicrystals. The Fibonacci sequence is a series of numbers in which each number is the sum of the two preceding numbers, and is represented in nature by the petals of a flower and the bracts of a pinecone.

Coherence in Consciousness — the Great Facilitator

It is the energy fields of fractal vectors that provide the information highway upon which consciousness travels. When coherence patterns are formed in these fields, you will experience déjà vu, synchronicities, and even miracles. Keep in mind that the energy of consciousness is the major player in helping to create this coherence.

Human thought forms, as a part of energy in consciousness, are some of the most influential of all energies in our cosmos, much greater than the combined energy of all the suns in our universe. This is because thought forms always contain consciousness, and consciousness is part of the original source energy for the existence of all that is.

Harnessing the power of your thoughts through meditation, contemplation, and prayer, combined with unconditional love and compassion, will facilitate the great change in global consciousness. This great change is simply a remembering of this universal truth — we are all one love.

We all originated from the same source of love that permeates everything and beckons us to reunite to create a new energy on earth. This new energy that will make war, famine, poverty, and strife something we only read about in history books, and will make us wonder — why did we wait so long?

So now that I've given you an overview of how it might be possible that the unified field of energy in our universe is conscious, let's move on to the Quantum Connection guided meditation.

To download the Quantum Connection Guided Meditation, go to www.mindinhealing.com/guided-meditations

Homework

The take-home message about emotional stress is that it always starts with your perception. So use present-moment awareness — mindfulness — to be aware of your perception of things.

Are things always what they seem? Absolutely not. Could you possibly change your perception? Yes! Practice changing your perception and see how you ratchet down the stress in your life.

Make a habit of viewing your life and experiences through the lens of energy. Think of everything as being some form of energy. Why? Because everything is energy. Is the energy you are experiencing nurturing you or taking you down? Do you need to eliminate or reduce some energy? Do you need to increase or add some forms of energy? I especially want you to think of food as energy, as that can be so helpful in making optimal food choices to improve your health.

Finally, practice the Quantum Connection guided meditation. Give yourself a week to practice this very powerful meditation before moving on to the next guided meditation. The Quantum Connection meditation technique will take you out of your monkey mind and reconnect you with your true self.

Believe it or not. :)

Chapter 6
The Science of Heart Consciousness

Introduction to the Heart Mind

THE HEART MIND IS THE consciousness of your heart.

Your brain sends instructions to all of your organ systems, but as it turns out, your body receives a lot of information from your heart. One very important function of your heart it to help regulate balance in your autonomic nervous system, the part of your nervous system that is on autopilot. The ability of your heart's consciousness to help regulate your autonomic nervous system is due to the fact that a significant proportion of autonomic nervous system changes are triggered by your emotions.

Emotional stress triggers the sympathetic arm of your autonomic nervous system, creating a cascade of events related to the fight-or-flight response. You can work with your heart mind, the consciousness of your heart, to power up the parasympathetic arm of your autonomic nervous system, which regulates relaxation, repair, and rejuvenation.

The HeartMath Institute teaches a technique of visualizing your heart space while imagining breathing through your heart. (45) Once you have done that, HeartMath says to conjure a high-energy emotion like gratitude, compassion, or love.

HeartMath has also published some groundbreaking research on intuition, but first let's review the two main types of intuition. Local intuition is what researchers say is related to pattern recognition and memory retrieval from your subconscious and conscious mind. Nonlocal intuition is something mainstream researchers don't touch with a ten-foot pole because they don't have a scientific explanation for it. That doesn't stop pioneering researchers at the HeartMath Institute from tackling it.

Nonlocal intuition is intuition you shouldn't have logically known and is not related to pattern recognition or memory retrieval. Nonlocal intuition sometimes contains information about the future. Woo woo, right? Not so fast. There's legitimate research on this topic, and I'll discuss it shortly, but let's first learn about the power of your heart mind.

A huge electromagnetic field emanates from your heart space, which is five thousand times stronger than your brain's electromagnetic field. (46) You can engage people with the electromagnetic field of your heart because, remember, energy contains information. By consciously moving your focus to your heart space, and intentionally opening up your heart's energy field of love, you can work with this energy to project it to others. When you connect with someone through your heart's energy field, you are coming from a place of love. This works because our body-mind is made of energy, and this energy can be projected with intention.

Have you ever had an experience where you walk into a room and not a word is said, but you can instantly tell if someone is enraged or happy, even if they have their back to you? I sure have.

I can tell you from experience that when you practice mindfulness and meditation, your awareness may increase to the point where you become highly sensitive to energies. This includes the energies of other people. These energies contain information, and when you hone and start trusting your intuition, you're able to interpret this information more accurately. I've already explained the changes that occur in your brain with long-term meditation practices. The areas of your brain associated with awareness start to thicken. This has the potential to translate into increasing your awareness of and interpretation of different types of energetic information.

Your body consists of multiple electromagnetic fields, and when these electromagnetic fields engage with someone else's electromagnetic fields, an exchange of information takes place. If you practice engaging these energies and interpreting this information through an increased sensory awareness, you'll get really good at it.

I predict that a few years from now we'll have the technology to take videos and pictures of this type of energetic exchange between people. For those of us who don't want to wait for that proof, you can start practicing engaging these energies now.

This is partly how nonlocal intuition works — you are engaging a field of energy that contains information. HeartMath research, which I discuss shortly, suggests that you first receive nonlocal intuitive information with your heart mind.

I encourage you to start engaging people with your heart mind. You'll find that when you do this, you'll begin to realize how powerful you truly are. Through this type of practice, you become more aware of how your presence impacts other individuals. This is because your presence contains energetic information. As you become more aware of this, it becomes easier to be mindful of what type of energy you bring into a room. Through regular practice, you'll see that the energy you create through intention produces shifts in others.

So here's something for you to try, and when you do this, I want you to keep a journal of the kinds of responses you get from people. The next time you are going into a meeting with someone that you typically have had an adversarial relationship with, practice bringing a heart-centered consciousness into the room before the meeting starts. Do whatever it takes for you to envision this in your mind's eye ahead of time. Some people will imagine filling the room ahead of time with pink heart-shaped balloons or cute puppies. It doesn't matter how you do this; just let your mind create some type of symbolic representation of love that resonates with you.

Then visualize the loving energy in your heart's electromagnetic field projecting out in front of you as you enter the room. As you sit down, envelop this person with your heart's electromagnetic field. This type of visualization strengthens your intention through coherence and helps create more powerful results.

By doing this visualization, you are setting a divine intention. Some consider this a form of prayer. When the time comes for your meeting, you'll feel a peace that surpasses all understanding. This peace comes from having your heart space open, and it will be very difficult for either of you to shift into an adversarial mode. You'll be amazed at how you change your experience with someone when you set this intention and do this visualization ahead of time.

Being Empathic with Healthy Boundaries

Someone once asked me, "What if your intuition works against you such that you are a sponge and you pick up everyone's energies?" Here is my answer: that can happen to people who are very sensitive, who are highly empathic. Use mindfulness and meditation to shore up your emotional foundation so that you are not "plugging in" to everyone. You can make a heart connection with people without plugging in. You can engage the energies of others with healthy boundaries.

The problem is that when you are a highly sensitive empath, you have an incredible amount of compassion and want to fix everyone by alleviating their suffering. Of course, this is unrealistic. When you try to alleviate all of someone's suffering, you "plug in" in an attempt to give him or her energy and make things better. Empaths may obsess over how to help another person while doing so without healthy boundaries. You'll have gone home where you should be spending time with your family, but you're still plugged in to that person you are trying to fix.

If you are an empath — a highly sensitive and compassionate person — use mindfulness and meditation to practice unplugging from people. Visualize yourself unplugging energetic cords from them while saying, "I'm unplugging. I'm unplugging." When you are successful in going into a deeper meditation and entering a slower alpha or theta brainwave predominance, you enter the realm of your subconscious mind. Your subconscious mind doesn't know the difference between what is real and what's not real, so when you do this type of practice, your new intention will eventually become your new reality. The more you practice this, the deeper those neuronal pathways become in your brain because of neuroplasticity. After a while you stop plugging in to people without healthy boundaries.

Plugging in to people without healthy boundaries is a bad habit. Many of us need to feel wanted. Some of us need to feel like we are always helping people, so we use that as an excuse to plug in to everybody. Next thing you know, you're exhausted because this habit has drained your energy. I understand this well because I used to have a habit of plugging in to people without healthy boundaries, but I finally realized how much suffering it was creating in my life. So I practice this unplugging visualization in my meditations when I catch myself pathologically plugging in to people.

You can make a choice through awareness to unplug. The more you practice unplugging, the more your subconscious starts to become okay with not trying to constantly alleviate everyone's suffering. In reality, you can still serve others by helping alleviate others' suffering, but you can now do it with healthier boundaries.

It takes practice, and you can take advantage of neuroplasticity to create these new neuronal pathways of being okay with not always plugging in to people.

Just go to that quiet place deep within yourself, and work with your subconscious to say, "No, that's not healthy for me. I'm not going to plug in to everyone and stay plugged in. I can still love them and connect with them, but in a healthier way."

The Amazing Power of Your Heart

Your heart has an independent brain and nervous system. Think about what happens when someone has a heart transplant. During a heart transplant, surgeons sever nerve connections to the heart, including the vagus nerve, and all of the spinal nerves. When surgeons place the donated heart into a transplant recipient's body, they do not reconnect any of these nerves. They don't need to because the heart has its own intrinsic nervous system — its own brain. The heart is able to function independently from the body's nervous system. The amazing heart is able to maintain a proper rhythm and continue to pump appropriate amounts of blood to the transplant recipient's body despite being cut off from the rest of their nervous system.

Your amazing heart is also an endocrine organ. It creates and releases hormones including atrial natriuretic factor and oxytocin. Your heart is not only capable of electrical self-regulation; it communicates hormonally with your other organs.

Atrial natriuretic factor is a hormone released by your heart when the atria, the top two chambers of your heart, are stretched.

Atrial natriuretic factor then goes to your brain, your blood vessels, your kidneys, and to your adrenal glands communicating that the volume of blood in your body is too high. This in turn causes your blood vessels to dilate thus lowering your blood pressure.

In addition, your heart releases a hormone called oxytocin. Oxytocin is the "love hormone," which is important for bonding with others. So your heart, which is symbolic of love, actually releases a love hormone.

Your heart also contains intrinsic cardiac adrenergic cells, which release the neurotransmitters epinephrine and dopamine just like those found in your brain. Your heart has its own brain, which releases neurotransmitters affecting your awareness and your intelligence. By intelligence, I mean heart intelligence.

When you work with your heart's energy field and its consciousness, or heart mind, by doing meditative techniques such as those developed by the HeartMath Institute, you help balance your autonomic nervous system. This is clinically proven to improve your cognitive abilities, make you smarter, more efficient, and a better test taker. (47)

The examples I've given you of the amazing power of your heart show you why it's so important to work with the consciousness of your heart mind through mindfulness and meditation techniques.

Heart Rate Variability Reflects Coherence

Heart rate variability is the beat-to-beat variation of your heart rhythm, and a healthy heart has a highly variable rhythm. When you experience what's called coherence in your heart rate variability, this is reflected by a beautiful sine wave pattern on heart rate variability analysis. Think of coherence as all of the instruments in a symphony playing in tune to the same beat.

Coherence in heart rate variability reflects balance in your autonomic nervous system, the part of your nervous system that acts as the autopilot for your body's functions. This coherence reflects balance in your autonomic nervous system and in your emotions because the two are intimately connected.

One thing that's really important about mindfulness and meditation is that these practices improve the way you regulate emotions. So by working with your heart mind through meditative practices, you create coherence in your heart rate variability, which helps balance your autonomic nervous system as well as your emotions.

The HeartMath Institute says that when you create coherence in your heart rate variability, you create coherence in all of your organs' systems. This is because when you shift your autopilot into a relaxed, smooth, and efficient state, your entire body becomes more efficient. This whole-body efficiency positively influences your overall health.

Nonlocal Intuition and the Heart Mind

The heart is an amazing organ with its own brain. It has the ability to receive and process information independently from the brain in your head. According to research by the HeartMath

Institute, your heart mind perceives without conscious reasoning. This means it can perceive information without the brain in your skull consciously reasoning through that information.

What their studies show is that your heart mind is the receiver of nonlocal intuition, which is intuition coming from outside of you that has nothing to do with memory retrieval or pattern recognition. This is possible because your higher mind is channeling this information into your heart mind from the unified field of energy, the universal mind, which connects everything and everyone. Your higher mind channels this information by processing energy, because as we know, energy is packed full of intelligent information.

The energy of the unified field contains infinite amounts of information because it contains the energetic information of everything and everyone. Your higher mind is connected to this unified field like an information highway, but instead of moving cars, it moves energy. Even the highway itself is made up of energy.

Creating Coherence

A study published by the HeartMath Institute shows how nonlocal intuition is received by your heart mind before your conscious mind. (48, 49) All the participants in this study were experienced practitioners of HeartMath meditative techniques. They could enter into what's called physiological coherence at will by using these meditative techniques, and they were able to produce coherence in their heart rate variability because they practiced these techniques on a regular basis.

The technique they used was to imagine breathing through their heart space. Then they conjured a high frequency emotion such as love or gratitude. This HeartMath technique first creates coherence in heart rate variability, which is the beat-to-beat variation in the heart's rhythm. Coherence in the electrical rhythms of the heart then translates into physiologic coherence throughout the rest of the organ systems of the body. This is like all of the woodwinds in the orchestra playing in tune and at the same tempo, followed by each group of instruments coming on line until they are all eventually playing in tune and at the same tempo. Part of the way you trigger physiological coherence is by conjuring and sustaining higher energy emotions such as love and gratitude.

HeartMath has developed devices to monitor heart rate variability by attaching a monitor to an earlobe or finger. When you create coherence in your heart rate variability using the HeartMath technique, you'll see this beautiful smooth sine wave pattern on a graph in HeartMath's software. Creating this coherence pattern in your heart rate variability results in increased synchronization between the two branches of your autonomic nervous system. This means that the two branches of your autonomic nervous system, which is the autopilot part of your nervous system, start to come into balance.

When doing meditation techniques that trigger your relaxation response, your autonomic nervous system begins to balance by increasing parasympathetic activity. The parasympathetic arm of your autonomic nervous system is integral to optimal health because it initiates repair, recovery, and rejuvenation. When you enter a state of coherence, you increase heart-brain synchronization resulting in your heart and brain working together and communicating more efficiently. This efficient heart-brain communication eventually translates into synchronization or coherence between all of your body's physiological systems.

Everything is made up of energy, including your body and mind. So when you do this HeartMath technique, you create coherence, not only in the energy systems of your heart and your brain, but throughout all of the energy systems of your body. This is because you are creating coherence, or balance, in your autonomic nervous system, which is your autopilot directing the activity of all of your organ systems without you consciously thinking about it. The end result is a more efficient and harmonious interaction of all of your body's organ systems.

The purpose of this study published by the HeartMath Institute in 2004 was to replicate a previously published study that demonstrated your body has the ability to respond to an emotional stimulus prior to you actually experiencing it. In other words, your body-mind is able to detect a future event. Whoa! Really? Yes, really.

In this study there were twenty-six adults — eleven males and fifteen females. All had previous experience with meditation, and all were experienced practitioners of the HeartMath emotional management technique. They could all enter physiological coherence at will because they had honed this skill by practicing HeartMath's technique. They were told that they were participating in the study to test their responses to different types of emotionally stimulating pictures and were unaware that the true purpose was to study nonlocal intuition.

Each person was randomly shown forty-five pictures on a computer screen in two separate sessions. In each session, they were shown thirty calming pictures and fifteen pictures that were designed to stimulate a negative emotional response. While they were viewing these pictures, they were continuously monitored by an electrocardiogram (EKG) to track their heart rates, and by an electroencephalogram (EEG) to track their brainwaves.

The first session was done at their baseline state, and the second session was done just after they had practiced the HeartMath technique of focusing on their heart by imagining breathing through their heart space while conjuring a high-energy emotion, such as love and gratitude. Researchers were aware that prior scientific studies showed that when someone anticipates seeing a picture that stimulates a negative emotional response, they experience an initial slowing of their heart rate. So it wasn't a surprise when this study showed the same reaction.

In this study, a greater slowing of heart rate occurred prior to the participants seeing the emotionally charged negative picture rather than the calm pictures. In fact, slowing of their heart rate occurred 4.75 seconds prior to the participants actually seeing the picture with their eyes. This slowing of the heart rate prior to the person seeing the negative picture reflects the receipt of nonlocal (coming from outside of their body-mind) intuitive information by the heart mind.

This nonlocal intuitive information notified their heart mind that an emotionally charged negative picture was coming

4.75 seconds before they saw it with their eyes. An EEG monitor assessing their brainwaves showed that there was a consistent shift in brainwaves 3.5 seconds prior to them seeing the emotionally charged negative picture with their eyes. This is consistent with their brain beginning to process this nonlocal intuitive information after processing it with their heart mind, but before they actually saw it with their eyes.

In review, this study showed that their heart mind received nonlocal intuitive information 4.75 seconds prior to the actual picture being seen by their eyes. Then their brain responds approximately one second later, followed by them seeing the emotionally charged picture 3.5 seconds later. The findings in this study were statistically significant and could not have been accounted for by chance.

What this study suggests is that your higher mind picks up and sends nonlocal intuitive information from the unified field of energy that connects everyone and everything. This nonlocal intuitive information is transmitted to your heart mind first.

In the second session — the one after which they had practiced the HeartMath technique and then viewed the pictures — females demonstrated a more significant heart rate response to the nonlocal intuitive information than males, meaning the females had more of a significant slowing of their heart rate prior to seeing the negatively charged pictures. This suggests that women may be more open to receiving nonlocal intuitive information than males after performing the HeartMath technique to create coherence in their heart rate variability.

HeartMath's conclusion was that there is strong evidence that nonlocal intuitive processing involves the body accessing the field of information that is not limited by the constraints of space and time. This means they were actually seeing into the future.

The take-home message is that by practicing creating coherence in your heart rate variability by the HeartMath technique, you potentially increase your ability to receive and process nonlocal intuition.

Emotions and Your Heart Mind

Emotions can shift your autonomic nervous system into either a stress response or a relaxation response depending on your overriding emotion. How well you manage your emotions is reflected in your heart mind by measuring heart rate variability.

Let me put the term "negative emotion" in context before I start discussing the heart mind technique for transmuting negative emotions. We all live on the earth plane — a very dense existence of duality. Depending on an individual's perception, this duality can be interpreted any number of ways. What may be a negative perception to one person may be nirvana to the next. So keep in mind that "negative" is contextual, so therefore I'll leave the definition of what is a negative to each individual.

I prefer the terms "high-energy emotions" and "low-energy emotions," with "high" and "low" representing both ends of the duality spectrum. What is most important is that even if an emotion is perceived as "negative" or "low energy," it should not be considered bad. Negative or low-energy emotions are actually good, because they help us to know when there is something in our lives that might need to be changed or healed. Negative emotions can simply serve as a marker that healing or change needs to occur.

While negative emotions can help create an imbalance in your autonomic nervous system, you can use the consciousness of your heart mind to help transmute these negative emotions. Unconditional love is an inherent part of your heart mind's consciousness and this powerful energy can be used to transmute or transform the energies of what you may perceive as negative emotions.

For this Transmuting Negative Emotions technique to be effective, you must first let yourself really feel the negative emotion. One problem is that people don't like feeling negative emotions so they find ways to distract themselves when they start to feel them. This distraction disrupts the proper sequence of events to effectively heal and transmute the negative emotion. Or some people may wallow in the negative emotion, so much so that they forget they have the power to transmute it.

If you don't work through a chronic unresolved negative emotion and instead keep it suppressed, it smolders within you as an unresolved emotional conflict. This unresolved emotional conflict creates a persistent stressor in your body-mind. A persistent emotional stressor, even at a subconscious level, may keep your autonomic nervous system in a chronic stress state of fight-or-flight. An autonomic nervous system in a chronic stress state eventually causes a breakdown of your body's systems, resulting in disease.

Sometimes people think they've worked through an emotional conflict, only to find that a situation in their life triggers it to surface later on. When you avoid feeling any chronic smoldering negative emotions or suppress them, then you may never psychologically resolve the underlying issue that originally produced that specific negative emotion. That smoldering negative emotional issue is always going to live in your subconscious mind so that it can easily be triggered and cause pain.

A classic example is the lack of forgiveness of a former spouse that triggers hate, anger, or a general unease every time there is a need to interact with him or her because of your mutual children. In this instance, your lack of forgiveness and the associated detrimental emotions that are triggered becomes a poison you intermittently sip the rest of your life. In addition, the significant negative impact that this scenario likely has on your children's health is something you might not have considered.

Transmuting Negative Emotions with Your Heart Mind

To begin the transmuting negative emotions technique, you have to first allow yourself to really feel the negative emotion, whatever that is for you. I'll have you imagine a person or an ongoing situation in your life that creates a stressful response for you. Then I want you to sit with it and really feel it.

When successful, this meditation technique shows you the power of your heart mind. If you sit with a negative emotion and do not run from it or be scared by it, you can work with your heart mind to process and release it. Or you can express it in a healthy way so that it resolves and no longer has a stressful impact on your body-mind.

This technique, when done properly, prevents a negative emotion from smoldering in your subconscious and conscious minds. This technique is, in essence, you engaging a deeper wisdom within yourself to work through and properly process the origin of a negative emotion. This technique has the potential to improve your health, especially when you master it and use it on a regular basis.

Transmuting negative emotions using the consciousness of your heart mind is a more advanced meditative technique, so be sure you have mastered the basics of mindfulness and meditation before attempting it. For this technique to be most effective, you should first master being still and quiet, fully engaging the present moment, and using diaphragmatic breathing to trigger a sustained relaxation response. By mastering these basics, you train your body-mind to maintain a peaceful presence even while fully feeling a negative emotion. Ultimately, it's about creating a balanced body-mind ecosystem.

Transmuting Negative Emotions

You can work with the consciousness of your heart mind to heal the parts of you that are wounded and you think can never be repaired. The ability to heal is in your power. You just have to believe. This technique is more likely to work if you open your belief system and embrace these concepts. This meditation technique is designed to transmute negative emotions, but you need to first sit with a negative emotion and accept it as a friend. This friend has something really powerful to teach you about yourself and what you are capable of.

When you perform this meditation technique, notice where you feel the negative emotion in your body. Because you are a body-mind, and not a separate body and mind, emotions often have a physical component that may manifest as tension or even pain. Emotions are intimately tied to physical sensations. When you experience a traumatic event, you may store emotional distress in certain areas of your body. Your subconscious mind memorizes every experience, and as the late Candace Pert, PhD, pointed out, your entire body is your subconscious mind.

In the Transmuting Negative Emotions meditation technique, after you sit with and feel the negative emotion, I have you notice where this negative emotion resides in your body. Then imagine breathing through that area of the body to initiate the energy of movement.

Then you make the negative emotion aware of the unconditional love of your heart mind. This reminds your body-mind that your heart mind is available with a huge store of unconditional love to pour into this area to help heal it. I then ask you to set an intention to be shown the circumstances surrounding the origin of this negative emotion.

The negative emotion may originate in your childhood, even though the negative emotion seems to be related to the animosity between you and your ex-spouse. As strange as that may seem, the true origin for the negative emotion you feel relating to your ex-spouse may have first been triggered in childhood. An example of this is a child who was abused by her father and learned that she couldn't trust a male figure who was supposed to love her unconditionally. She then ended up marrying a person that reminded her of her father as a subconscious attempt to heal the relationship with her father.

This is a very complex topic, so don't overthink it; just go with what your subconscious mind shows you. When you are shown the origin and circumstances of the original event that helped create a negative emotion, you can then use a higher awareness to process and release it. You are empowered to do so by having been shown the bigger picture and how the pieces of the puzzle fit together. For example, by forgiving her father, she is able to forgive her ex-husband, and he no longer triggers this negative emotion.

By staying fully engaged with this technique while in a sustained relaxation response, you have the potential to enter into the realm of your subconscious mind to see the true origin and circumstances of the negative emotion. If you are ready to see it, you'll be shown the circumstances through a higher awareness, and then have the option to let it go or transmute it. Transmuting the negative emotion often requires forgiving yourself or someone else, which will be much easier to do while in a sustained relaxation response.

A key issue regarding healing an old emotional wound is that you have to be ready to let go of judgment of the circumstances surrounding the origin of the negative emotion. Another key issue is that if you are not ready to let it go, then don't force it. Stop the process and go back to mastering the basics of mindfulness and meditation. When you have shored up your body-mind by mastering the basics of mindfulness and meditation, you may come back to the negative emotion and be ready to heal it at that time. Always listen to what your body-mind tells you, and this listening gets easier by mastering the basics of mindfulness and meditation.

If you insist on holding on to the idea that someone hurt you and that you'll never be able to forgive them, then don't bother attempting this technique at this time. But you need to be aware that by figuratively holding on to something like that, it has detrimental effects on your body-mind in more ways than you could ever imagine. I guarantee you that if you hold a lack of forgiveness, it is negatively impacting your body-mind in some way.

You may say, "No, that's not bothering me. I just hate them." You definitely have the option to believe that, but that's a perfect example of a belief that's not a truth. That belief is slowly eating away at your body like termites devouring the structural foundation of a house, and you don't know that it's happening until a wall gives way and you get sick. Your lack of forgiveness represents the termites. Because you are a body-mind, emotional influences have a significant impact on your physiology.

Even if you aren't ready to release an old emotional wound through forgiveness, you can put a toe in the water by just considering that possibility. I read a quote somewhere that said lack of forgiveness is like drinking poison and expecting the other person to die. When you forgive someone, you are not justifying their behavior, but removing a burden from your body-mind so you can rebalance and become healthy on many levels.

Mastering Heart Mind Consciousness

Another easy way to help transmute negative emotions is to keep a gratitude journal. When you record in your journal what you are grateful for, you shift your consciousness into the space of gratitude, which is a high-energy emotion. I've discussed what high-energy emotions do to your physiology — they create a shift in your heart rate variability, balancing your autonomous nervous system, which translates into better health.

Starting a gratitude journal doesn't mean you have to write a novel. You can choose to just write one thing you are grateful for each day, and do that for a week. If you decide after a week that process is helping to create a positive shift in your life, then you might decide to do it longer. Keeping a gratitude journal shifts your awareness toward the good things happening in your life, and is especially powerful if your current perception is that a lot of bad things are happening in your life.

In addition, I challenge you to practice sending love to people with your heart mind, including strangers. I usually do this when I see a homeless person, because they trigger compassion in me to send them love. An important component of this technique is to release judgment of them and their situation. We actually have no idea what others have gone through that might have resulted in their current situation. Many people have experienced emotional and physical abuse as a child, which alters the brain and contributes to poor coping skills, which may lead to homelessness. (50)

These strangers don't have to know you are doing this, and you can do it from afar without getting in their space or plugging in. You might be surprised what happens when you start doing this. I've found that this technique hones my compassion for others and triggers within me a state of gratitude for all of the blessings in my life. Talk about creating good energy!

Negative emotions are powerful teachers and, optimally, should be welcomed with open arms. The healthy expression of negative emotions is very good for you. It is when these negative emotions get trapped in the tissues of the body, and are not expressed, or processed and removed, that dis-ease occurs.

Know that every experience and emotion you have in your life is for your highest good, that, if you pay attention, these experiences and emotions will teach you something about your life and yourself. That can be a powerful catalyst for growth and transformation. Your heart mind reminds you that it's okay to fully feel every negative emotion, as long as you express it, process it, and release it.

Spectrum of Human Emotion

Fear, anger, grief, and frustration, and other low-energy emotions represent a spectrum of the human experience, and are not something we should run from or avoid.

To heal a negative emotion, especially if it's one that has become chronic and is causing physical dis-ease in the body, such as pain, you've got to first allow yourself to feel the negative emotion. This is so that your subconscious mind and your heart mind can align to give you insight and a higher awareness about the original experience that created it.

Through the consciousness of your heart mind, you have at your disposal the powerful energy of pure unconditional love, inherent in which is unlimited forgiveness, which you can use for self-healing. Your heart mind reminds you that you are an all-powerful spiritual being with an unlimited ability to love and heal.

Unresolved Emotional Conflict

A life experience may be so traumatic that it creates a fragmentation of your psyche and locks a negative emotion into your body and mind. This is what I call an unresolved emotional conflict.

In my practice, I've seen time and time again that unresolved emotional conflicts prevent healing of longstanding health conditions. Because of the inability of the psyche to resolve the original emotional trauma, the associated negative emotion lodges in the body-mind, and creates a chronic interference field.

This chronic interference field is the stagnant energy of an unresolved emotional conflict. Any interference field in the body-mind has the potential to disrupt the optimal flow of energy and create physical dysfunction. Often this dysfunction manifests as pain or some other physical disturbance resulting in disease.

Unresolved emotional conflicts can be removed, just like any interference field in the body, through the use of energy. Remember: everything is energy, including your thoughts as consciousness.

Transmuting Negative Emotions Technique

This Transmuting Negative Emotions technique uses the energy of the consciousness of your subconscious mind to let you view the circumstances of the originating event with a higher awareness. Once you view the original trauma with a higher awareness, you have the ability to change your perception of the original trauma, thus initiating the healing process.

This technique also brings in the consciousness of your heart mind to show you how to finalize the healing with the energy of unconditional love. Inherent in unconditional love is unconditional forgiveness, which is often required to heal an unresolved emotional conflict.

Shamanic Wisdom of the Heart Mind

Ancient shamanism describes a healer who has the wisdom to take a mystical journey, find the missing parts of someone's fragmented soul, and make them whole again.

With this technique, I'm asking you to be your own shaman. As your own shaman, you are taking a mystical journey inward, finding the missing fragments of your psyche, and piecing them together so that you can be whole again.

With the wisdom of your heart mind, you are empowered by seeing the bigger picture of this experience and intuitively are given clues on how to effectively express the emotion, process it, and release it. But you must first invite the negative emotion to sit with you as a friend, a friend who has a powerful and loving message.

To download the Transmuting Negative Emotions Guided Meditation, go to www.mindinhealing.com/guided-meditations

Homework

Practice the Transmuting Negative Emotions with Your Heart Mind guided meditation. If you find that when you attempt this guided meditation, you experience difficulty, I recommend you put this meditation technique aside until you have mastered the basic concepts of mindfulness and meditation. These basics include diaphragmatic breathing, engaging present-moment awareness, and inducing a sustained relaxation response.

If you have significant difficulty attempting this advanced meditation, it means you need to build a better foundation first. You need to get really good at being quiet, still, and relaxed while being fully in your body. This is like developing any new skill, such as learning to play a musical instrument.

If you decide to purchase the HeartMath software or app, you'll need to use it on a regular basis to understand how your body is responding to your mindfulness and meditation techniques.

I recommend you keep a gratitude journal for a week, which can be as simple as writing down each day one thing you are thankful for. Don't make it a chore, or you won't do it. I recommend you write down each day three things you are thankful for. Gratitude journaling helps you refocus your conscious thoughts on positive things, which shifts your energy in a positive way. Give it a shot. You'll be amazed that such a simple concept can create such a big shift.

Practice sending love to people with your heart mind. They don't even have to know you are doing it. I especially would like you to try this on someone who consistently triggers a negative emotional response in you. This could be your boss or manager, or someone you love. In certain instances, you'll see such a dramatic response that you'll think surely it was a coincidence. Hmm. Was it?

Have fun with this!

Chapter 7
Your Subconscious Mind
and Brainwave States

Subconscious Mind

YOUR SUBCONSCIOUS MIND IS A memory bank for all of your life's experiences. Your subconscious and conscious minds even encode your experiences while you are in the womb. (51) This is because your subconscious mind is like a supercomputer that has the potential to memorize every experience you've had in your entire life. This is important to understand because your subconscious mind is running on autopilot in the background of your conscious mind and is playing a major role in how you filter your current experiences. This filter includes associated beliefs and emotions linked with these experiences and, therefore, has more of an impact on your daily life than you might realize.

Your subconscious mind is always running on autopilot and helps regulate what you are not consciously aware of. This means it is constantly working in the background, but it doesn't have to wait on your conscious mind to play a role in how you respond to a situation. You may have automatic responses to different situations you encounter, with the predominant response originating from your subconscious mind.

This is where mindfulness comes into play and why mindfulness is so valuable. When you practice mindfulness and meditation, you get really good at raising your awareness about your current experiences. This higher awareness lets you override automatic reactions triggered from your subconscious mind.

Your subconscious mind and your autonomic nervous system are related in that they are both on autopilot and constantly functioning outside of your conscious awareness. Because of this, their responses are automatic. Your autonomic nervous system is the part of your nervous system that regulates everything that you are not thinking about, such as breathing, heart rate, sweating, and blood pressure.

Because your autonomic nervous system and your subconscious mind are so intimately related, your subconscious mind and its associated beliefs and emotions can affect your physiology. A classic example of this is a panic attack that comes out of the blue despite you feeling fine and not consciously worrying about anything. For no apparent reason, you might suddenly develop a rapid heart rate, sweating, and a feeling of anxiousness, though you have no idea what caused your anxiety and its associated physical symptoms.

From a subconscious perspective, this could be because your subconscious mind was filtering your experiences, and picked up on subtle clues that reminded it of a prior traumatic experience.

These reminders can be as simple as a song, an odor, or even the clothes someone was wearing. While you didn't consciously make the connection with those subtle clues, your subconscious mind did, and triggered your autonomic nervous system to initiate a warning in the form of palpitations, sweating, and anxiousness.

Introduction to Brainwaves

An electroencephalograph (EEG) is a device that measures and records brainwaves, which reflects the electrical activity of your brain. The electrical activity of brainwaves is measured in frequencies as hertz (Hz), or cycles per second, ranging from fast to slow. You'll never be in just one brainwave state as there are multiple types of brainwaves occurring throughout the brain at various times. When you begin to have a predominance of one brainwave state over the others, you'll start to experience the effects associated with that predominant brainwave state.

Brainwave States

Your brain's activity always contains a mixture of different types of brainwaves, but when one type of brainwave becomes predominant, you can take advantage of that specific brainwave predominance to manipulate consciousness. One example of this is using meditation to create a predominance of slower brainwaves such as alpha or theta brainwaves to work with your subconscious mind to facilitate healing of old emotional traumas.

Gamma Brainwaves

Gamma waves are fast brainwaves, between 27–100 Hz cycles per second. A predominance of gamma brainwaves is associated with enhanced creativity, language processing, memory, and being in the flow. You've probably experienced a flow state when working on a project and become so entrenched in the experience that you lost track of time and achieved incredible productivity.

Athletes often experience flow states when they are excelling in their sport. Some may remember everything happening as if in slow motion with incredible efficiency. These types of efficient flow states are what you may experience when your brain emits a predominance of gamma waves.

In 2004, neuroscientists attached EEG monitors to long-term Buddhist practitioners and found that during meditation they not only exhibited a predominance of gamma waves, but that their gamma waves were synchronized in multiple areas of their brains. (52) This study showed that regular meditation can result in an unusual control over the brain's ability to synchronize its function, and synchronized brain function has the potential to translate into even more incredible efficiency.

Beta Brainwaves

The next fastest are beta brainwaves, which can be categorized into fast beta and slow beta. Faster beta brainwaves in the 20–31 Hz range are generally associated with stress and anxiety. Slower beta brainwaves in the 13–21 Hz range are generally associated with alert states of concentration and focus with increased energy.

Alpha Brainwaves

As your brainwaves slow even more, you'll produce alpha brainwaves in the range of 8–12 Hz. Alpha brainwaves occur when you close your eyes and start to relax. These brainwaves are associated with a reduction in pain and anxiety, and are important for deep meditation and the ability to effectively work with your subconscious mind.

Theta Brainwaves

As brainwaves slow toward the lower end of the alpha range, you may start to feel so relaxed that you get sleepy. Then as your brainwaves slow even more and you get even more relaxed, you'll start to produce theta brainwaves in the 4–7 Hz range.

The periods when you are starting to wake up and starting to drift off to sleep are one of the best times for using positive affirmations. This is because when you are in a predominance of alpha and theta brainwaves, it's possible to plant positive affirmations into your subconscious mind.

If some positive affirmations just don't feel right to you, then the core belief associated with those affirmations may not be a part of your belief system. Or this may indicate that you've got a limiting belief system stuck in your subconscious mind preventing you from believing a positive affirmation.

Later, I'll show you a technique for using positive affirmations, which is designed to work best with a predominance of alpha and theta brainwaves. The reason I want you in a predominance of alpha and theta brainwaves during this technique is so that you can go into your subconscious mind and remove any limiting beliefs. Working with your subconscious mind is much easier when you are in a sustained relaxation response associated with a predominance of deep alpha and theta brainwave states.

Theta brainwaves in the 4–7 Hz range are associated with being very relaxed and when starting to drift off to sleep. They are associated with light dreaming, hypnagogic states, and even deeper meditations. Theta brainwave states are ideal for doing self-hypnosis and for working with your subconscious mind. You may notice that when you have a predominance of theta brainwaves during meditation, your state of consciousness becomes dreamlike, though you are still aware that you are meditating.

It will be tempting to fall asleep when you enter a theta brainwave predominance because it is so relaxing. When you feel like you might fall asleep, bring awareness to your original intention to enter a deep meditation, and be curious about what comes up. If you do fall asleep, it's okay. It just means that you've entered into a state of delta brainwave predominance.

Delta Brainwaves

Very slow delta brainwaves are in the 0.2–3.5 Hz range and are associated with sleeping. When you have a predominance of really slow delta brainwaves, dreaming will cease. Your brain's production of delta waves is important for getting a good night's sleep. Production of sustained delta brainwaves is also important because deep sleep increases your parasympathetic tone allowing for your body to regenerate, recover, recuperate, and rebalance. Deep sleep is also a time when your brain starts to literally take out the trash and detoxify itself.

Brainwave Entrainment as a Meditation Tool

Brainwave entrainment has been around for very long time. One example of ancient brainwave entrainment that's still used today is drumming. Drumming at a set frequency such as in the alpha wave range will entrain your brainwaves into the alpha frequency if you listen to it long enough.

If you pay attention long enough to any type of repetitive stimulus, your brain may start to entrain to the frequency of that stimulus. This repetitive stimulus may be in the form of sound, light, and vibration.

Modern brainwave entrainment technology uses binaural beats and isochronic tones set to a specific frequency. These beats and tones when embedded into sound tracks for meditation are heard as a repetitive stimulus. Different frequencies are used depending upon the goal of the meditation track.

It's common to use frequencies that will entrain brainwaves down into the alpha and theta range to help someone relax or deepen meditation. A delta frequency in the form of auditory binaural beats or isochronic tones may be used to help someone fall asleep.

Clinical Benefits of Brainwave Entrainment

In 2008, researchers performed a systematic review of the medical literature regarding the psychological benefits of brainwave entrainment. They reviewed twenty-two studies and concluded that brainwave entrainment is a legitimate therapeutic tool. (53)

One study in this review looked at children with Attention Deficit Hyperactivity Disorder (ADHD) and stimulated them with brainwave entrainment frequencies in the alpha and beta range. They found that those children had significant increases in standardized reading test scores.

Another study in school-age children with ADHD found that when they stimulated them with frequencies in the 12–14 Hz range, they had approximately a 70% improvement in their behavior. Another study used a combination of theta and delta frequencies in people with anxiety and found that it resulted in significant reductions in their anxiety.

The conclusion of this systematic review is that brainwave entrainment reduces pain, including tension headaches and migraines; helps improve premenstrual syndrome, and improves behavior in children with certain learning disorders, and attention deficit disorders.

A more recent pilot study suggests that listening to binaural beats in the theta brainwave range is effective in reducing the perceived level of pain for people with chronic pain conditions. (54) Brainwave entrainment, while not widely used, is a proven therapeutic tool for certain individuals with certain health conditions.

Binaural Beats

One type of auditory stimulus used in modern brainwave entrainment is binaural beats. Binaural beats use two tones of slightly different frequencies played in the right and left ear, resulting in the brain perceiving these different frequencies as the difference between the two. For example, if you want to use binaural beats to entrain someone into the alpha range (8–12 Hz), play one tone in one ear at a 108 Hz and another tone in another ear at a 100 Hz, and the brain will perceive it as the difference between the two, which is 8 Hz. Since this 8 Hz is played as a repetitive stimulus, the brain will start to entrain to this frequency and you'll likely develop a predominance of alpha brainwaves.

Headphones are necessary for binaural beats to be effective because each ear has to receive the different tone. In the brainwave entrainment industry, binaural beats are often embedded in music tracks. This is because listening to repetitive tones by themselves can be irritating to some people.

Isochronic Tones

Isochronic tones are another type of repetitive auditory stimulus commonly used in brainwave entrainment music tracks. Isochronic tones, unlike binaural beats, use only a single frequency tone that is played in both ears at the same time in a repetitive manner. This repetitive tone is set to a specific frequency depending on your goal for that specific brainwave entrainment session. For example, if you want to entrain brainwaves in the theta range, you might choose a tone set to a frequency of 5 Hz, and play it as a repetitive stimulus in both ears at the same time. In most commercially available tracks, you just choose a track based on whether it's entraining to gamma, beta, alpha, or theta brainwave ranges.

Isochronic tones tend to be more effective than binaural beats partly because your brain doesn't have to analyze the difference between two frequencies. With isochronic tones, you are simply supplied with a repetitive frequency in both ears at the same time.

Choosing binaural beats or isochronic tones boils down to personal preference. I personally prefer binaural beats over isochronic tones because I find isochronic tones to be slightly irritating, as I hear them more prominently than binaural beats. Some may prefer the increased auditory prominence of the isochronic tones, especially if they find them more effective in shifting their brainwaves. Unlike binaural beats, isochronic tones do not require headphones to be effective.

In the end, using brainwave entrainment audio tracks is a way to diversify your meditation practices. It's also a way to take advantage of modern technology to help shift your brainwaves to achieve a desired intention with your meditations. I personally use brainwave entrainment tracks to achieve deeper meditation states by facilitating a predominance of alpha and theta waves in my brain. In doing so, I've been able to work with my subconscious mind to heal old emotional wounds and find and remove limiting beliefs.

In the next chapter, I walk you through a process of finding and removing limiting beliefs. This meditation technique is considered an advanced technique, and to be most effective, requires that you first master the basics of mindfulness and meditation. These basics include being still and quiet, fully engaging the present moment, using diaphragmatic breathing to trigger a sustained relaxation response, and dropping into a sustained alpha or theta brainwave predominance.

Chapter 8
Belief versus Truth

EVERYONE HAS BELIEFS, AND HOPEFULLY, you always remain open to changing your beliefs. This openness to changing your beliefs leaves room for personal growth and evolution. Staying open to changing your beliefs doesn't mean you have to change them, just that you stay open to that possibility.

As you evolve and grow throughout your life, it becomes necessary to leave certain beliefs behind. This is because not every belief is a truth. Just because you strongly believe something doesn't make it true. An example of this is beliefs related to prejudice. Prejudice is associated with a certain set of rigid beliefs, usually associated with stereotyping, and often passed down from generation to generation. Rigid beliefs regarding stereotyping lead to harmful behaviors, despite these beliefs not being true.

Stereotyping is about making generalizations, and it's impossible to accurately generalize about every group of people, because each individual in that group has unique attributes.

Discernment, which is intimately tied to intuition, is required to know if a belief is a truth. Intuition strengthens and improves when you regularly practice mindfulness and meditation. Discernment improves because mindfulness and meditation increases the gray matter in areas of your brain associated with attention, self-awareness, and sensory processing.

Your ability to accurately intuit something is enhanced by improving your attention, self-awareness, and the accurate processing of sensory information. Being able to accurately intuit something is a powerful tool for accurate discernment. Accurate discernment, strong intuition, mindfulness, and meditation all increase your emotional intelligence, which is the ability to recognize and properly manage your emotions and the emotions of others.

Improved discernment increases your ability to differentiate a belief from a truth. Beliefs that are not true are called limiting beliefs because they inevitably limit you in some way. Limiting beliefs can literally be stuck in your subconscious mind. Your subconscious mind doesn't care whether something is true or not. It's like a computer program that is programmed to make you believe, and thus act, in certain ways regardless of the truth.

So if a limiting belief is stuck in your subconscious mind, its programming effect is to limit you and possibly sabotage your life experiences and your relationships. Limiting beliefs prevent you from living your life to the fullest.

Limiting beliefs can originate at any time in your life, but commonly, limiting beliefs originate in childhood and become stuck in your subconscious mind. This is because from birth to about age seven, your brain is incredibly neuroplastic. During this time, your brain is very malleable, and you also don't have a clear concept of cause and effect. This combination of enhanced neuroplasticity and impaired cause-and-effect reasoning makes it more likely for a limiting belief to develop and then get planted in your subconscious mind.

Primitive cause-and-effect reasoning in early childhood may increase your risk of false assumptions and generalizations, especially during times of traumatic experiences. For example, children of divorced parents may blame themselves as the reason why their parents divorced, even though the children had nothing to do with why their parents split up.

Questioning Your Beliefs

The following are three questions you can ask yourself to help discern whether your belief is a truth or not. Consider a belief that you hold very strongly, and then ask yourself these three questions. This works better if you contemplate the answers to these questions rather than quickly and reflexively answering.

1. Does this belief serve my highest good?

"Highest good" implies a higher spiritual order of good. This also implies selflessness, which considers the best interests of not only yourself but also others.

2. Is this belief holding me back in any way?

Answering this question accurately requires a lot of self-honesty, so contemplate how this belief may be limiting you in any way in your life.

3. Do I absolutely know this belief is true?

This third question is a tough one because we don't absolutely know a lot of things. If you contemplate the answer while setting an intention to be completely honest, you're much more likely to answer it accurately.

Using Positive Affirmations as a Starting Point

Another method to help you discern whether a belief is a truth uses positive affirmations as a starting point. I give you a list of core positive affirmations in Appendix 2 of this book. These are affirmations that everyone should believe to have a healthy psyche. Examples of core positive affirmations include:

- "I love myself unconditionally."
- "I forgive myself unconditionally."
- "I accept myself unconditionally."

These core affirmations are what everyone should believe to have good self-esteem and a happy life. The optimal way to use these affirmations is to say them out loud while looking in a mirror. If you are uncomfortable saying them while looking in a mirror, simply say them out loud to yourself.

Some people may laugh at this technique because it reminds them of the *Saturday Night Live* skit of Stuart Smalley saying, "I'm good enough, I'm smart enough, and doggone it, people like me." I used to laugh at that skit, but believe it or not, there is incredible wisdom you can tap into by effectively using that first set of affirmations.

When you say these affirmations out loud, be aware of how each one makes you feel. If saying them doesn't resonate with you, or if you feel some type of negative charge in your body-mind when you say them, this may indicate you hold a limiting belief in your subconscious mind regarding that affirmation.

Now take whatever affirmation doesn't resonate with you and say it in the reverse, and this gives you a limiting belief with which to work. For example, the positive affirmation would be "I love myself unconditionally," while the limiting belief would be "I don't love myself unconditionally."

If you used core affirmations to determine your limiting belief, the core belief rephrased as a negative statement will also create resistance or tension in your body-mind. This is because intuitively you know there is an associated limiting belief regardless of whether you phrase it positively or negatively.

Now take the phrase, which represents your limiting belief, into a deep meditation, preferably dropping down into the alpha or theta brainwave state to uncover its origin. This will take you becoming and staying very relaxed in your meditation to create a predominance of sustained alpha and theta brainwaves while doing this technique.

By dropping into a predominance of alpha and or theta brainwaves while setting an intention to uncover the origin of your limiting belief, you enter the realm of your subconscious mind. When you enter the realm of your subconscious mind, you're much more likely to accurately see and understand the circumstances around which the limiting belief was formed. By seeing the circumstances surrounding the origin of the limiting belief, you develop a higher awareness around the limiting belief, which ultimately enables you to release it.

Removing Limiting Beliefs Technique

When doing a deep meditation to uncover and then release a limiting belief, you need to set a very specific intention to release it, and then to get very relaxed to enter the realm of your subconscious mind. Setting this intention with your conscious mind cues your subconscious mind to cooperate with this process.

Then use some type of meditative practice to drop your brainwaves from the analytical beta brainwave predominance down into the slower alpha and theta brainwave predominance. Transitioning to this slower brainwave predominance can be achieved through any meditative practice or combination of practices that triggers a deep and sustained relaxation response. I recommend you use a combination of diaphragmatic breathing and binaural beats or isochronic tones embedded in music tracks to achieve this type of sustained deep relaxation.

You'll know you've reached an optimal brainwave state for working with your subconscious mind when you feel deeply relaxed, and you may even feel like you are dreaming but still awake. For novice meditators, or people who don't meditate on a regular basis, obtaining this slower brainwave predominance isn't terribly difficult to achieve. It just takes practicing something that your body-mind already knows how to do, which is to deeply relax.

Once you begin to get good at deeply relaxing, it gets easier and easier to go into this meditative state the more you practice it. The reason it gets easier to enter this state of deep relaxation with regular meditation is because of neuroplasticity — your brain's ability to create new neuronal pathways through repetition.

When using core positive affirmations to determine underlying limiting beliefs, I recommend you say each core affirmation out loud while looking in a mirror. Go through the list of core positive affirmations and put an "X" by the ones that don't feel right. Knowing which affirmations don't feel right takes being mindful of your body and mind while you are saying them.

Then choose an affirmation that doesn't feel right and turn that affirmation into a negative statement that represents your limiting belief. For example, if "I love myself unconditionally" is an affirmation that doesn't feel right, turn it around, and it says, "I don't love myself unconditionally." This represents your limiting belief, which you can take into your meditation to find out why it's there, process it, and release it.

Enter into a deep meditative state by relaxing into a sustained alpha or theta brainwave predominance. You'll know you've entered into an alpha wave predominance when you feel very relaxed. You'll know you've entered a theta wave predominance when you feel like you are about to drift off to sleep, and your thoughts become dreamlike, but you're still awake. Then set an intention to understand the circumstances around the development of that limiting belief. When you bring this limiting belief into an alpha or theta brainwave state of deep relaxation, you enter the realm of your subconscious mind. Remember that your subconscious mind is functioning on autopilot at a level of awareness below your conscious mind. You can more easily enter the doorway of your subconscious mind by combining deep relaxation with the curiosity of a child.

Why do you want to enter the realm of your subconscious mind to find and remove limiting beliefs? Because your subconscious mind remembers everything and it has the potential to reveal the truth about those memories. This is a reason why deep meditation as a form of self-hypnosis may aid you in seeing and removing limiting beliefs. Accessing your subconscious mind to understand the truth about an experience, especially if it was traumatic, lets you bypass primitive aspects of your brain and nervous system that help lock a limiting belief into your body-mind.

The idea is to look into your subconscious mind to see the original event, which triggered the limiting belief through some type of psychological trauma. By trauma, I mean an event that triggered a sympathetic nervous system mediated fight-or-flight response that helped lock this memory into your body-mind. When you experience a traumatic event, a primitive mechanism of protection by dissociation may occur during the fight-or-flight response. This dissociation may create a schism in your body-mind, which prevents you from seeing all of the circumstances surrounding that original event.

Your body-mind may remember this situation a certain way, including associated perceptions and beliefs that may or may not be true regarding the circumstances. Regardless, it becomes locked into memory, and from that point forward, similar events may arise in your life to trigger that old memorized fight-or-flight response.

This is an example of what shamans describe as fragmenting of the soul. Shamanism teaches that during trauma, a part of the soul leaves the body to survive the experience. In this definition, the soul represents the vital life force of the person. There is a lot of symbolism here, but the general theme is that trauma may create a schism, or fragmentation of the psyche, creating a state of dis-ease, from that point on, if the original experience is not processed properly. From the point of the original unresolved emotional conflict, that person may experience a lack of vitality relating to that original traumatic experience, and this lack of vitality may express itself as emotional and physical illness.

Why is it important to develop a higher awareness surrounding the circumstances of the original event? Because when you see the circumstance of the original event with a higher awareness, false or limiting beliefs associated with it will be revealed. The truth becomes known, and at that point, you have a choice to view it differently, allowing yourself to process it and release it.

Healthy processing often involves the energy of unconditional love, whereby you are able to conjure compassion and forgiveness regarding the original event. Processing the traumatic experience with a higher awareness lets you retrieve that fragmented part of your soul, or life force, which helps restore your vitality, and prevents another triggering of your fight-or-flight response related to the memory of that original trauma.

Once you dive into your subconscious mind with a higher awareness to accurately see the originating event and circumstances that helped create a limiting belief, then you are able to discern the truth about that situation.

Beliefs are associated with emotions, which trigger your nervous system to react in a certain physiologic way. Ideally, you want to go to the original psychological source of the limiting belief to most effectively deal with it. What I have personally experienced, as well as what I have heard from people who do this technique, is that it is commonly an experience in childhood that is the origin of a limiting belief.

When you set the right intention and use a meditative technique to enter the realm of your subconscious mind, the origin of the limiting belief may be shown to you. This is because your subconscious mind, just like a super computer, remembers everything.

Once you see the original event and the circumstances surrounding it in a deep enough meditation to enter your subconscious mind, you develop a higher awareness of the circumstances that triggered the limiting belief. The development of limiting beliefs is often related to the triggering of a stress induced fight-or-flight response from the sympathetic arm of your autonomic nervous system.

When you develop a higher awareness of circumstances surrounding that original event, this lets you discern the truth in that situation. Discerning the truth lets you release a limiting belief. When properly done, this technique is very powerful and highly effective. At first glance, it may seem like a very esoteric technique, but by actually doing this technique, you'll come to understand exactly how it works.

This Removing Limiting Beliefs technique works much better when you memorize the process and take it into your own meditation at your own pace. I recommend you listen to the guided meditation a couple of times, and then once you understand the process, do the technique at your own pace in your own meditation.

This technique may not be as effective for you when done as a guided meditation, because I don't know when you need to pause and process something. This is because your mind is going to show you different things at different times, and I don't know when those times are for each individual. You can listen to the guided meditation to understand the process, but I highly recommend that you do this meditative technique on your own at your own pace.

If this technique is not something you feel comfortable doing, then absolutely don't attempt it. This is an advanced type of meditation technique that should only be attempted after you have established a stable emotional foundation. This includes having established a solid mindfulness and meditation practice whereby your emotional intelligence has increased to the point where you are emotionally stable and are able to sustain a peaceful presence throughout the process.

What shouldn't happen during this technique is that you remember a stressful event and it triggers your autonomic nervous system as a stress response. That's why mastering the basics of mindfulness and meditation before you attempt this is very important. You should first master diaphragmatic breathing, and being fully present in your body while at the same time triggering a sustained relaxation response.

Finally, do not attempt this technique if you are emotionally unstable, have had a recent traumatic experience, or are adjusting to psychiatric medication. I can't emphasize enough that this removing limiting beliefs meditation technique should only be attempted if you are emotionally stable. If you have any doubts whatsoever, you should first speak to your doctor or mental health counselor before attempting it. In fact, I recommend that you work with a licensed physician or mental health counselor if you have any underlying mental disorder.

Summary of the Removing Limiting Beliefs Technique

Get very relaxed in the meditation.
Say the limiting belief to yourself.
Recognize where you feel the tension in your body.
Recognize the associated emotion.

Ask your subconscious mind and higher mind to align and show you the circumstances surrounding the origin of this limiting belief.

Allow this information to bubble up from your subconscious mind. It's important that you stay relaxed when your subconscious mind begins to send this information. This is because deep relaxation creates coherence for this energetic flow of information to be smooth and efficient.

When you become aware of the origin of this limiting belief, you now have a higher awareness that lets you choose if you want to release it.

If you are ready to release it, set an intention to let it go and imagine blowing this limiting belief and associated emotion out of your body through your heart area.

This technique is similar to the Transmuting Negative Emotions technique, though this one is more in depth, and requires a more sustained relaxation response.

To download the Removing Limiting Beliefs Guided Meditation, go to www.mindinhealing.com/guided-meditations

Homework

Practice using brainwave entrainment technology to deepen your meditations.

Practice questioning your beliefs.

Practice using core affirmation to identify your limiting beliefs.

Practice removing your limiting beliefs.

Chapter 9
The Mind as Healer

Your Inner Physician

YOU HAVE AN EXQUISITELY POWERFUL and infinitively intelligent healing system residing within your body, which is your inner physician. Your inner physician has proven itself to you over and over in your life when your body has healed itself without outside intervention. Your inner physician is much more capable when your body is properly supported, and research on the placebo effect proves the power of your mind in triggering your inner physician to heal yourself.

The Placebo

In a clinical study, a placebo is a substance containing no active ingredient, or a sham procedure that doesn't involve any active treatment. A study published in 2002 involved one hundred eighty patients with osteoarthritis of the knee, and proved the power of the mind in healing the body. A two year follow up found that the patients who had the sham procedure with only small incisions made on their knee without any actual arthroscopic procedure did just as well as patients who underwent an actual arthroscopic surgery. (55)

The regulatory gold standard for testing the medical effectiveness of a medication or a medical device is a randomized double-blind placebo-controlled clinical trial. 'Placebo controlled" means a placebo is being used as a control to help test for the true effectiveness of the real medication or procedure.

It's kind of crazy, if you think about it. For a new drug to be approved in the United States, it either has to be shown as effective and safe as a previously approved drug, or has to be shown to be safe and more effective than a sugar pill. In other words, medications often simply have to be safe and beat the power of the mind in order to attain regulatory approval to treat a specific condition.

The paradox is that placebos can be as effective, if not more effective, than real medicines or real procedures. This drives researchers crazy, because when they believe they have a very effective medication, and a clinical study shows a sugar pill works better, they're not happy. Most researchers don't understand why this happens, but the latest research on the placebo effect provides major clues.

Power of Belief

So how can a sugar pill be as effective, or more effective, than a pharmaceutical drug? It ultimately boils down to belief.

Your belief about a pill or a procedure triggers a very specific physiologic response in your body. The power of your mind, or the power of your belief, triggers your inner physician to turn on and heal yourself. The evolving research on the placebo effect is so amazing that a special center affiliated with Harvard Medical School has been created to study the placebo, and some researchers all over the world are committing their lives to studying the placebo effect. That's because placebo effect research is providing major scientific evidence for what the ancients taught — the mind is a powerful healer through the power of belief.

Placebo Effect

The placebo effect is a psychobiological phenomenon, meaning it has both psychological and biological effects. This is in keeping with the fact you are a body-mind and not a separate body and mind. There is no separating the two.

Scientists say the placebo effect starts in the brain, but it actually starts in the mind through consciousness. Your brain is an organ that helps manage consciousness but it's not the only source of consciousness. The placebo effect always results in some type of clinical improvement and it's intimately tied to the ritual of the therapeutic act.

Ritual of the Therapeutic Act

The ritual of the therapeutic act is an integral component of the placebo effect and includes all of the components of any type of therapy. This includes personal beliefs and expectations of the patient, memories about prior therapies, the sights and sounds of health professionals, hospitals, other healthcare facilities, and any type of medical instrument. It also includes interactions with other patients, and whether or not a needle or another type of device touched you. It even includes the color, shape, and smell of medications. But most important, it includes the words spoken by doctors and other healthcare practitioners. These words are important because they include seeds of hope and expectation for positive outcomes.

Nocebo Effect

The nocebo effect is the exact opposite of the placebo effect. It also begins in the mind and triggers the brain to respond, but unlike the placebo effect, the nocebo effect has a negative effect on your physiology, resulting in clinical worsening.

The nocebo effect is also related to the power of belief but is triggered by negative suggestions and negative expectations. Let me give you an example of the nocebo effect. A participant in a clinical trial is given a placebo and is read a list of potentially negative side effects. They then experience one or more of those side effects as a nocebo effect. Despite being given a pill containing no active substance, the participant experiences an adverse reaction related to being read a list of side effects. This is a nocebo effect.

Placebo Effect and Your Brain

Magnetic resonance imaging (MRI) shows that placebos consistently turn on certain parts of the brain and cause the release of very specific neurotransmitters. Scientific studies show that when a patient is given a pain medication, and then the pain medication is replaced with a placebo, but the patient is told they are getting the pain medication, their brain releases a specific neurotransmitter depending on which pain medication they were originally given.

Morphine, an opioid agonist, causes neurotransmitters called opioids to be released in the brain. If a patient is given morphine, and the morphine is taken away, and then they are given the placebo but told it is morphine, that placebo causes their brain to release opioids. In the case of non-steroidal anti-inflammatory drugs like ibuprofen, they don't cause a release of opioids in the brain; they cause the release of cannabinoids in the brain. So if a patient is given ibuprofen, and then ibuprofen is taken away, and they are given a placebo and told it's ibuprofen, the placebo causes the release of cannabinoids in their brain.

Placebo effect research proves that the body memorizes the effect of a medication, and then if you are given a placebo, but think it's that medication, your body then reproduces the exact physiologic effects of the original medication.

Placebo Effect Quantified

The placebo effect can be quantified, meaning a placebo's effectiveness can vary depending on the type of information given to the patient when they take the placebo. A fascinating study shows that not only can you quantify a placebo's effect based on the information you give with it, but that all medications contain a placebo effect. This study showed that by increasing the amount of positive information you give with a medication or a placebo, you incrementally boost the effectiveness of both the medication and the placebo. (56)

The study, published in 2014, took 66 migraine headache patients and gave them a pill each time they experienced a migraine. They were either given a placebo or a medication for migraines called Maxalt. The pills were labeled three different ways — placebo, Maxalt, and placebo or Maxalt. Depending on how the pill was labeled, it created information that varied from negative to neutral to positive.

Whether patients received placebo or Maxalt, increasingly positive information in the way the pills were labeled incrementally boosted the effectiveness of both placebo and Maxalt. For example, when the placebo was labeled Maxalt, it was more effective for treating migraine than when it was labeled placebo. And when Maxalt was labeled Maxalt, it was 50% more effective than when Maxalt was labeled placebo.

Researchers concluded that whether the treatment involves medication or placebo, the information given to the patients, and the ritual of pill taking are important components of care.

Placebo Effect and Your Immune Response

A clinical study published in 2002 was the first to show that immune suppression can be behaviorally conditioned by placebo in humans. (57) Conditioning is a learning process that occurs due to association. In this study, healthy young men were conditioned over three days by being given a distinctly flavored drink paired with Cyclosporine A pills. Cyclosporine A is a medication used to suppress the immune system, and blood testing confirmed that their immune systems were indeed suppressed.

Their immune systems were allowed to recover, and after about a week, they were given the same distinctly flavored drink, but this time it was paired with placebo pills. Guess what happened? The placebo pills paired with the flavored drink suppressed their immune system to the same degree as when they were given the flavored drink plus Cyclosporine A.

Their bodies had been conditioned by their prior exposure to the flavored drink plus the Cyclosporine A. During that prior conditioning, their bodies had memorized the physiologic effect of the immune suppressing medication and simply reproduced that effect based on associating it with the flavor of the drink. Your body will literally memorize the physiologic effect of any medication and reproduce that effect when conditioned. In this case, the drink's flavor simply acted as a trigger to produce a physiologic effect that their bodies had memorized.

Placebo Effect and Parkinson's Disease

Parkinson's disease is a degenerative disease of the nervous system in which the brain doesn't release enough dopamine. This lack of dopamine results in tremors and muscular dysfunction associated with muscle rigidity. Parkinson's disease is treated by giving medications that stimulate dopamine release.

In a study published in 2001, Parkinson's patients were told they would either get an injection of a dopamine agonist to help stimulate the release of dopamine in their brain, or they would get an injection of a placebo. Despite being told they might get a placebo injection, all of the Parkinson's patients who got a placebo injection had at least a 200% increase in dopamine release, and 50% of them had concomitant motor improvement. (58)

It's pretty amazing that you can positively impact a disease like Parkinson's disease with a placebo. In fact, placebo research on other Parkinson's disease patients has shown similar responses. (59) This is yet another dramatic example of turning on someone's inner physician based on the power of belief.

Psychology of the Placebo Effect

Here I show you how to hack the psychology of the placebo effect to make it work for you in mindfulness and meditation.

Research clearly shows that expectation plays a role in the placebo effect, so you can use expectation in your meditation to facilitate your own placebo effect.

Before you begin meditating, set an expectation for being well emotionally and physically. Then bring this expectation into your meditation. Remember that your subconscious mind doesn't know the difference between what is real and what isn't real. When you go into a deeper brainwave predominance of alpha and theta waves during meditation, you are accessing your subconscious mind.

By bringing a solid expectation for wellness into deeper brainwave states during meditation, your subconscious mind becomes conditioned to this new reality. By conditioning yourself to a new reality in your subconscious mind, you are much more likely to have a shift in your physiology to help create that reality.

In addition, placebo effect research shows that positive expectations reduce anxiety. (60) When you bring an expectation of getting well into deeper brainwave states and begin to feel that possibility as a reality, you reduce anxiety, which automatically increases parasympathetic tone in your autonomic nervous system. This increased parasympathetic tone initiates repair processes and reduces cortisol levels, all of which results in rejuvenation and rebalancing.

If you truly believe in your expectation of getting well, you'll definitely reduce your anxiety and help condition your body-mind so that your inner physician turns on to heal you. Placebo effect research bears this out.

Placebo effect research also shows that when you have an expectation for reward, you anticipate being rewarded by getting well. But if you've got limiting beliefs stuck in your subconscious mind that say you don't deserve a reward, or you don't deserve to get well, that limiting belief may block your inner physician placebo response.

As previously discussed, you can use affirmations to test for limiting beliefs that may be stuck in your subconscious mind. For example, say to yourself "I deserve to be rewarded," or "I deserve to be well." How do those statements feel to you? Do they feel right? Do you resonate with those affirmations? If those statements don't feel right — if those statements create a negative feeling or negative charge in your body — then I suggest you use the Removing Limiting Beliefs meditation technique outlined in this book. That technique lets you find and then remove limiting beliefs stuck in your subconscious mind that may be hindering your body's ability to heal.

When you remove subconscious limiting beliefs involving being well, the Inner Physician guided meditation I introduce at the end of this chapter will be more effective for you. In the Inner Physician guided meditation, I walk you through a technique where you expect to get well, which requires an unhindered belief that you can get well.

I use the scientific evidence in placebo effect research to back up the specific suggestions given in this meditation. This isn't just about thinking happy thoughts and positive thinking. Science actually shows that your thoughts, and especially your beliefs, clearly impact your physiology. So take advantage of your inner physician and do these techniques to help you get clear on what you truly believe so that your positive beliefs can help heal you.

The main reason I'm explaining all of this science in placebo effect research is because it may take you actually knowing the science to convince yourself of the power of your beliefs and thoughts over your physical body. After all, the placebo effect boils down to your belief; and if you know the science and the facts about self-healing, it can power up your belief system around your ability to self-heal.

I want to clarify that I'm not asking you to ditch your doctor and think that you can do all of your healing by yourself. It's ultimately about striking a balance with what you are capable of at any point in time and using external resources that you have available to address any diseases you may have. I'm asking you to balance your stress-related negative thoughts with the power of the positive thinking so that you are more likely to actually improve your health or completely heal. I also encourage you to integrate positive thinking, prayers, affirmations, meditations, and the power of positive belief into any treatment regimens directed by your physicians.

I told you earlier about conditioning associated with the placebo response. Conditioning means learning through association, and you can maximize your conditioning related to the placebo effect by conditioning yourself in your meditations.

You can use certain mantras, music tracks, or guided meditations while you are meditating to help you visualize and feel yourself being completely well. When you do this, your mind begins to associate the mantra or the music with you actually being well. From that point forward, your body's physiology shifts into wellness mode when you say those mantras or hear that music. As you know from the science outlined in this book, your physiology shifts all the way down to how your genes turn on and off.

Placebo Effect and Social Learning

Another psychological component of the placebo effect is social learning, which relates to you healing because you see or hear of others being healed. This is well established in placebo effect research on pain. (61) So I encourage you to read about others who have healed from serious diseases, including terminal diseases like stage IV cancers.

See Appendix 3 of this book for resources on social learning and spontaneous remission.

Reinforce Expectations

Reinforcing expectations is another powerful psychological aspect of the placebo effect. You can use mindfulness to guard against negative thoughts and beliefs regarding your health, which will indirectly help reinforce your expectation for being well. It's almost impossible to guard completely against negative thoughts, because a lot of negative thoughts are triggered from your subconscious mind, which will bubble up even before you are fully aware of it. But by using mindfulness, you can mindfully recognize when they do bubble up, label it as a thought that isn't necessarily a truth, and then let it pass before it triggers any significant negative impact on your physiology. This is a skill that requires practice, but as you continue to meditate and practice mindfulness, you'll get better at this.

Reinforce your expectations of being whole and well in your meditations by staying as positive as you can about your belief of being well. I'm not asking you to be in denial about what's going on with your health, and I'm not asking you to ignore health issues. This concept is about living a balanced life so that you regularly reinforce your expectations for wellness in real time.

Finally, when you assign meaning to something, you power up the potential for that something to have a major influence in your life. If something has no meaning to you, then it's really no more than a passing thought. If you assign positive meaning to it, especially a deeply intense positive meaning, that something becomes a belief that has the potential to be your truth.

When you intensely feel something with all of your heart, and when being completely healthy becomes a truth for you, your body-mind will help make it so. So, assign a deep positive meaning to your vision of being completely well and healthy in your meditations — body, mind, and spirit.

Placebo Effect and Attitude

Attitude is a very important issue when it comes to magnifying the power of belief in the placebo effect. Optimism plays a role in maximizing positive outcomes associated with the placebo effect. If you are an optimist, you are much more likely to experience a placebo effect resulting in a positive impact on your physiology. (62)

If you are prone to pessimism, you can use mindfulness to be more aware when you are being pessimistic, and then use the power of your mind to practice being optimistic. This may take a little practice, but when you practice being optimistic, the neuroplasticity of your brain kicks in to create deep neuronal pathways of optimism. A major benefit of becoming an optimist is that it increases your chances of experiencing placebo effects resulting in multiple health benefits.

The reverse is also true. If you are a pessimist, you increase your chances of experiencing a nocebo effect; meaning, if you have a negative attitude, you are much more likely to experience a negative physiologic reaction to medications and beliefs. (63)

Inner Physician Guided Meditation Technique

This guided meditation is about you believing that you can heal your body. I've already presented the science that supports your ability to heal yourself, so you know that you can do this. It starts with an intention to activate your inner physician — your inner healer. This is a process that occurs by aligning all your systems of repair, recovery, and rejuvenation.

All of your organ systems participate in this repair process, as it is the perfect ecosystem when properly supported. Trust that your inner physician knows exactly what to do to heal you. It's an innate intelligence.

It's also important that you hold a state of gratitude during this meditation to maximize your inner physician's power. In your mind's eye, see your body healed and perfectly whole, but here is the kicker — you must let it be in divine timing. Timing is the part of this process you don't necessarily have any control over.

The Power of your Belief Maximizes Your Inner Physician

Your body contains an exquisitely powerful inner physician that is always working on your behalf to keep you healthy. You can ramp up your inner physician's power through your thoughts and beliefs. The latest research on the placebo effect proves this fact beyond a shadow of a doubt. Based on the science I've presented thus far, you now know that your inner physician is capable of great feats of self-healing, especially when you believe that fact.

Your subconscious mind doesn't know the difference between what's real and what's not. You can take advantage of this fact while meditating to direct your inner physician to heal you.

The Intention

While participating in the Inner Physician guided meditation, make being completely well your current reality in your mind. And practice it over and over. When you do that, your body responds to your belief by creating positive shifts in your physiology.

When you memorize the vision and feeling of being completely well and whole, you are conditioning yourself to that reality. As I've explained, conditioning is an integral part of how the placebo effect turns on your inner physician.

Research on the placebo effect shows how your physiology shifts based on your beliefs. In this case, you are creating a whole new reality in your mind about being healed, complete with feelings and beliefs. Your physiology can't help but respond.

When you are going through the Inner Physician guided meditation, see yourself healed and whole in your mind's eye. See yourself being completely well, whatever that means to you. It's very important that when you see yourself being completely well, you feel what it feels like to be completely well.

I'm asking you to believe and trust, not in what I'm saying, but in what your mind is capable of, which is backed by science. Bring in the expectation of being completely well and healthy. Reinforce this expectation through repetition in your meditations.

When you truly believe in the power of your mind to turn on your inner physician, you will expect reward. This expectation of reward automatically reduces your anxiety around the concept of whatever dis-ease you may have.

This process of creating trust in your mind balances your autonomic nervous system by reducing sympathetic output and increasing the parasympathetic output of your autonomic nervous system. This triggers your inner physician to repair, rejuvenate, and rebalance, resulting in healing.

Reinforce your expectations for getting well in real time by living a balanced and healthy lifestyle, and your body will respond in kind. Eat healthy, get moving, and follow the directions of a qualified healthcare provider that you resonate with. Claim your power over illness and take full responsibility for your health.

Taking full responsibility for your health involves a lot of courage, but remember that you're not alone. Your family and friends support you and your healthcare providers are assisting you by mentoring you through this process. Despite all of their assistance, it's ultimately up to you which actions you take regarding your health. So take charge and start using the power of your mind to fully assist in the process of becoming whole and healthy.

There are people living on this earth who have experienced complete spontaneous remission of stage IV metastatic cancers. While this is not considered common, it does happen. People call this a miracle, but no one is immune to miracles.

The Process

Believe that you can heal your body.

Set an intention to activate your inner physician.

By fully relaxing into this guided meditation, your body's systems start to align and work together to repair, recover, and rejuvenate.

Trust that your inner physician knows exactly what to do.

Hold a state of gratitude for your inner physician's power.

It is very important that you allow your body to be healed in divine timing. Don't put any expectations on the timing, because if you do, you set limitations on and parameters around this process. That will only put you in a state of resistance to "what is," which triggers your stress response and defeats the whole purpose of this process.

Finally, understand that people can heal without being cured. When someone heals without being cured, they go into a state of pure acceptance of "what is" despite whatever disease or illness they may have. And for many, that is enough, because of the indescribable peace inherent in the process of complete surrender to the divine flow of life.

To download the Inner Physician Guided Meditation, go to www.mindinhealing.com/guided-meditations

Homework

Bring the power of belief into your life. This requires trust in yourself and your abilities.

Belief makes things happen! I hope I've provided enough solid scientific evidence to prove to you that belief absolutely makes your physiology change in dramatic ways. Take advantage of this! It just requires that you believe.

When doing the Inner Physician guided meditation, practice fully engaging the belief part, which facilitate the process of healing your body and mind.

Most important, be patient with yourself, because patience is a form of self-love.

Chapter 10
Higher Mind

YOUR HIGHER MIND IS THE component of your consciousness that extends outside of your physical body into the unified field of information that connects everyone and everything. Your higher mind is your spiritual channel, and as a spiritual channel, it is unlimited in divine wisdom and unconditional love.

Your higher mind only knows the truth, and aligning your higher mind with the consciousness of your heart, your heart mind, turbocharges your nonlocal intuition. This alignment also moves you from a state of fear to a state of love. In transitioning from lower energy fear to higher energy love, you open up unlimited energetic pathways to facilitate the flow of information.

Albert Einstein once said, "The intuitive mind is a sacred gift and the rational mind is a faithful servant. We have created a society that honors the servant and has forgotten the gift." Einstein was an absolute genius and recognized the importance of intuition.

Intuition, especially nonlocal intuition, is a sacred gift, because when you channel nonlocal intuition, you are tapping into a field of divine energy. This unified field of divine energy that connects everyone and everything is packed with information, and this information can be used to improve your life in numerous ways. The way you tap into this field of infinite divine energy as information is through your higher mind.

The concept of intuition in the medical literature is mostly discussed as local intuition, which is defined by intuition confined to the brain, and derives from pattern recognition and memory retrieval.

Nonlocal intuition is a knowing unexplained by logic, and does not originate in the physical body. It derives from your higher mind and the unified field of energy that connects everyone and everything.

Nonlocal intuition is truly sacred as it involves tapping into a spiritual aspect of our consciousness that is not scientifically explained and can only be experienced. Many of us have had intuitive experiences that could not be explained by memory retrieval or pattern recognition. Some people have even had nonlocal intuitive experiences but refused to accept it for what it was, because that experience did not fit into their belief system.

I encourage you to open your mind and allow yourself to experience nonlocal intuition. Some people are born with a gift of easily tapping into nonlocal intuition, but we all have this ability. It just requires you to believe and then practice aligning with your higher mind through meditation and mindfulness.

As a physician trained in the scientific method, I understand it pretty well. As a human being with an open mind who has personally experienced phenomena I can't scientifically explain, I also understand that science does not have all of the answers. Science is limited by the current technology available to us at this point in time.

The sacred god of science is also heavily influenced by personal bias, even in some of the most well designed scientific studies. So because of that, I have to combine a little philosophy with science in an attempt to explain the unexplainable. Let me tell you about a crazy experience I had that can't be fully explained by science.

Nonlocal Intuition in Action

I often go to Sedona, Arizona, a place I consider very spiritual, due to its unique natural settings. I love nature, knowing it is chock-full of divine energies. Sedona has some of the most beautiful red rock hills in the world and is a mesmerizing place to behold. When I go to Sedona, I set an intention to connect with the divine, and so it was no surprise to me that it was here where I was introduced to some supernatural energies of the divine.

On my first ever visit to Sedona, I met a beautiful, loving, and highly spiritual person named Nataya. Nataya is a clairvoyant artist. When she paints, she goes into a flow state by aligning with the spiritual channel of her higher mind and she gets messages. These messages for whom she is doing the painting contain spiritual information that she can't logically know. Nataya is unconditionally loving and nonjudgmental and her intention is pure. Because of this, the messages she receives are pure and full of unconditional love. In some way, these messages are meant to facilitate her clients' highest purposes in life.

Nataya calls these types of in-the-flow paintings "totem paintings," as she resonates strongly with Native American spirituality. So while she was doing my totem painting, which turned out to be a butterfly, one of the things she said to me was "I see you going to Germany to get a medical device." I thought to myself, "Okay, but I don't have any plans to go to Germany."

The End Result

I returned home, went back to work at my primary care clinic, and was working the evening shift. There was a family practice resident working that evening who is a good friend of mine to this day. He came up to me at the end of the shift, and said, "Hey, I hear you are into alternative medicine," and I said, "Yes. Are you?" Daniel, who is German, told me that his parents have an alternative medicine clinic in Germany. I later found out that it is a world-class alternative medicine clinic that draws patients from all over the globe.

As we were chatting, he wrote down two website addresses on a piece of paper and handed it to me. One was the web address for his parents' clinic, and the other was a web address for a pulsed electromagnetic field device, which his father helped prototype. Over the next few days, I studied both of these websites, and then began an intensive PubMed search to see if there were any peer-reviewed research articles on low-level pulsed electromagnetic field therapy. To my surprise, there were hundreds of published studies, with the bulk of these studies showing beneficial effects on animals and humans.

Shortly thereafter, I purchased the device and incorporated it into my medical practice with good results. So Nataya's message to me was mostly correct, with a minor issue being that I didn't go to Germany to get a medical device. Germany came to me. :)

My use of and writings about this device later led to me being asked to speak at multiple medical conferences for the American Academy of Anti-Aging Medicine. In essence, Nataya's channeled message helped facilitate my higher purpose by expanding my tool chest as a practicing clinician. Her message also helped lead me to teach large audiences at medical conferences, which was a major goal of mine.

Divine Synchronicities

The series of coincidences I just described can't be explained by chance, so I call these synchronicities. In my opinion, synchronicities have some type of divine facilitation. How could Nataya have known that I was going to incorporate some type of German medical device into my practice? There is no way she could have concocted that message to me based on memory retrieval from her subconscious mind or through cognitive pattern recognition.

Our Universe is Teeming with Energy

That message came to me via Nataya's higher mind — a spiritual channel from the divine unified field that connects the energies of everyone and everything. If you look out into this unified field with the naked eye, you'll see lots of empty space. The paradox is that there is no empty space in our universe, because all space is teeming with energy. This is because our universe originated as energy, which is the story of the Big Bang Theory.

According to scientists, a few seconds after The Big Bang, our universe was nothing but intensely hot energy particles and gases. As our newly birthed universe began to cool, mass started to form, and planets were created. I don't want to take anything away from the spiritual component of the birth of our universe. Ultimately, it's at the merger of science and spirituality where we're going to find the true answers.

All Energy Contains Information

The higher mind is where the energies of the earth plane merge with the energies of the spiritual plane. These energies contain information, including information from the unified field as divine messages to facilitate our higher paths in life.

Ask any scientist who studies energy, and she or he will tell you that all energy contains information. Examples of this are how the sun's rays contain energy, which tells receptors in the leaves of plants to initiate photosynthesis, and tells receptors in our skin to initiate the production of vitamin D.

Ultimately, it all boils down to energy to theoretically explain how scientifically unexplainable phenomena happen in our universe. More important, the revelation that consciousness is energy goes a long way in explaining parapsychological phenomena and even life after death. Our universe is energy based, and because of that, we are all energetic beings. When you, as an energetic being, learn to work with and channel these energies, you can do some amazing things.

The Intuitive Mind

Let me give you another example of my experience with nonlocal intuition, except in this case, my higher mind channeled the message. Intuitively, I had always thought that clairvoyance might be possible, and this was confirmed by my experience with Nataya's message regarding the German medical device. At that point, the ability to be clairvoyant became part of my belief system, and as such, I was about to experience my first profound experience as a clairvoyant.

In the fall of 2009, I started a complementary medical clinic in Jacksonville Beach, FL. Shortly after I opened the clinic, I received a call from someone named Brenda, a licensed massage therapist trained in craniosacral therapy. She told me that she had heard about my clinic, read my website, and was interested in working with me. I didn't know who Brenda was, but I asked her to come by the clinic and demonstrate her skills on me. I wanted to see if she would be a good fit for the clinic. So she came to the clinic, and what follows is an experience with my own clairvoyant ability.

As I lay there on a massage table, I began drifting into a deep meditative state. Based on my education and experience with meditation, I knew there was a predominance of theta waves occurring in my brain. It was so peaceful, an almost dreamlike state, and I could feel the wonderful effects of endorphins being released in my body.

Just as I felt myself drifting off to sleep, I heard "Andy, Andy," and then I heard "Andy's sister." Hearing this pulled me to a slightly higher level of consciousness, which stopped me from falling asleep. I let myself be pleasantly curious about what I was experiencing, and then I heard it again. "Andy, Andy," and "Andy's sister." This voice wasn't male or female; it was just there, but very adamant. I made a mental note to ask Brenda about Andy once we were done, and then I drifted off to sleep only to be awakened by the sound of my own snoring.

After I got dressed, I met Brenda outside in the waiting room, and I asked her, "Do you know a guy named Andy?" Brenda said, "No, but my best girlfriend in Maryland is named Andy." It kind of takes your breath away when you have an experience like that, and then I said, "What's going on with Andy's sister?" Brenda responded, "Her sister just entered hospice with end-stage breast cancer."

This is one of many nonlocal intuitive experiences I've had in my life. In this instance, it was via personal clairvoyance. Nonlocal intuition is one of the great mysteries in life that is so unexplainable, professional skeptics weigh in by saying that the possibility doesn't even exist.

I'm an advocate of healthy skepticism, which is a key part of the scientific method. The truth is that the scientific method is limited by the technology and methods through which it is applied. Just because we don't have scientific evidence for something, doesn't mean it doesn't exist. A lot of skeptics sometimes forget that part of the equation in their quest for truth through a lens of academic arrogance.

As a physician board certified in internal medicine who graduated with honors from medical school, I understand and appreciate the scientific method. I also appreciate the great mysteries in life, and am humble enough to admit the possibility something does exist even when I don't understand it. More important, when I do have an experience that defies logic, I'm going to do my best to try and come up with a rational explanation for how it might have occurred, however silly it may sound.

When someone who is mentally sound has a personal experience that defies logic, they know it happened because it was their experience. So when I hear someone say that the parapsychological phenomenon of nonlocal intuition doesn't exist, I remind myself that they have either never had the experience, or they had a nonlocal intuitive experience, but the phenomenon is just not part of their belief system.

It's your choice what to believe, but if you take skepticism to the point of cynicism about nonlocal intuition, it shuts you out of very real experiences that have the potential to empower your life. After all, having powerful intuition lets you become your own authority on many levels.

The third book of the Yoga Sutras described siddhis, or supernormal powers, that can be attained through meditation. These powers, such as clairvoyance, are actually normal powers of every human, and can be honed through various mind-body practices.

Most people who have nonlocal intuitive experiences write them off as coincidences, when in reality, those experiences involve simply tapping into the unified field, the energetic field of information available to us all.

The method for tapping into this energetic field of information varies from individual to individual. Some people, such as legitimate psychics, are naturally good at it. Other people have to work at honing this skill, but everyone is capable of it. I don't consider myself a psychic, but I've had multiple experiences like this.

If you want to sharpen your skill of tapping into the unified field of information, I suggest the following:

First, truly believe this is possible. Belief produces resonance, which facilitates an alignment of energies for an optimal exchange of information to take place.

Know that you are an energetic being in a universe that is made up of energy, and that all energy contains information.

Eat healthy and exercise regularly as these practices support the energies of your physical body. Food is energy, and the study of epigenetics shows that the phytonutrients in food literally turn your genes on and off to create wellness or disease.

Regularly do some type of mind-body practice, such as mindfulness and meditation, as this helps you to focus your energies for tapping in. When you practice mindfulness and meditation, you are creating coherence in your body's systems and training your consciousness, which is energy, to align.

Set the intention for your higher mind, also known as your higher self, to align with the layers of consciousness contained in your physical body.

Get really good at triggering your relaxation response, which is the opposite of your stress response. Triggering your relaxation response with any mind-body practice causes your autonomic nervous system, your autopilot, to go into a state of balance. You can trigger your relaxation response by simply belly breathing instead of chest breathing.

Set an intention to receive nonlocal intuitive information when you do these practices.

And finally, practice, practice, practice.

Belief, intention, and trust are the keys to being successful at this.

Aligning with Your Higher Mind

Aligning with your higher mind is part of the process outlined in the Power of the Mind guided meditation found at the end of this chapter. You start by setting a divine intention to align with your higher mind. After all, everything starts with an intention.

When you set a divine intention, you are calling upon the divine to facilitate this process. Here is the technique. First, acknowledge you are a spiritual being. By doing so, you acknowledge that you are an infinite being, which has unlimited potential. Then see yourself as an energetic being. As an energetic being, you are able to align the energies of consciousness to optimize a flow of information and power. Then set an intention to tap into the unified field of consciousness — the divine, unified field that connects everyone and everything.

Connecting Your Higher Mind with Your Heart Mind

Once you have aligned with your higher mind, set a divine intention to align the energies of your higher mind with your heart mind. This lets you channel infinite wisdom of the divine unified field into your heart mind. Visualizing a stream of energy connecting your higher mind with your heart mind facilitates this process.

How will you know when you are aligned with your higher mind? It will feel like unconditional love. There will be no fear and you will have no doubt. This part may take a little practice because you've got to quiet your mind to access this state of feeling rather than thinking.

Sealing the Deal

Sealing the deal is about enhancing the alignment of your higher mind with your heart mind through gratitude. When you align your higher mind with your heart mind, which is facilitated by visualizing a stream of energy connecting the two, you begin to feel unconditional love. This feeling encompasses a deep knowing, incredible inner peace, and trust.

Then you seal the deal by conjuring a feeling of profound gratitude. How can you not feel gratitude when you are feeling unconditional love? Know that you can trust this nonlocal intuitive information you are receiving when you feel a deep love and trust in the message.

You may need to regularly practice this technique to get really good at. Some will master the process quickly and feel the love more easily than others. If when you practice this process of aligning with your higher mind, you at first don't feel much love or trust, then I recommend you go back to practicing the basics of mindfulness and meditation. These basics include being still and quiet while fully present in your body during diaphragmatic breathing.

I recommend that you don't try to force the advanced meditation techniques until you have mastered being fully present in your body while in a very relaxed state. This mastery of peaceful present-moment awareness requires regular practice of the basics of mindfulness and meditation. If you attempt to force the advanced techniques before you are truly ready, you'll get frustrated, which defeats the process. If frustration occurs when you attempt the advanced meditation techniques, just go back to the foundational basics of mindfulness and meditation.

In summary, the Power of the Mind guided meditation is about aligning with your higher mind and connecting to the unified field, which brings the information contained in it down into your body to merge with the consciousness of your physical body.

To download the Power of the Mind Guided Meditation, go to www.mindinhealing.com/guided-meditations

Final Comments

It's important that you understand the difference between healing and curing. You can be healed without being cured. This type of healing involves coming into a place of acceptance about things you cannot change. When you do this, you enter into a peaceful state of nonresistance. Coming into this place of acceptance through nonresistance is often the first step in true healing. This sounds like a paradox because it is. Paradoxes are inherent in life and embracing them holds the key to deeper wisdom and empowerment.

I hope you've enjoyed this book. The techniques taught here need to be practiced with patience to be most effective. Be kind to yourself, and don't give up on working with these concepts and techniques. This patient practice can make a dramatic difference in your life.

Your mind is incredibly powerful so use regular mindfulness and meditation to hone its amazing abilities. I wish all of you the very best on this wild and exciting journey called life.

If you have any questions, please contact me through my website at www.Dr-Holden.com. Just know that I can't give any individual medical advice. If you liked this book, and I hope you did, please recommend it to your friends.

Appendix 1

Feeling Grounded Guided Meditation Transcript

Take a deep, relaxed breath in, and a slow, relaxed breath out.

Take another deep, relaxed breath in, and a slow, relaxed breath out.

Take one more deep, relaxed breath in, and a slow, relaxed breath out.

In your mind's eye, see yourself standing on a large grassy field.

The grass is the greenest green you have ever seen.

The sky is a vivid blue, and there are white, fluffy clouds floating by.

The sun is shining warmly on your face, and there's a cool breeze blowing on your skin.

The air smells fresh and clean.

Now, become aware of your feet standing solidly on the earth.

The earth is here to support you.

Now, imagine your feet growing roots down toward the center of the earth.

Deeper and deeper, until these roots reach the center of the earth and wrap around its core.

You feel a slight tug on your feet and are reminded the earth is here to support and ground you.

Now, imagine a white light coming down from the cosmos in through the top of your head, down through your body, and connecting to the roots at your feet.

You are fully aligned with and supported by the energies of our beautiful universe.

Take a slow, deep, relaxed breath in, and a slow, relaxed breath out.

Take another deep, relaxed breath in, and a slow, relaxed breath out.

Take one more deep, relaxed breath in, and a slow, relaxed breath out.

You are feeling safe and secure, loved and connected, grounded and at peace.

You belong and have a right to be here.

You feel stable and secure in this world.

You have a complete and sustaining trust in life.

There is abundance for everyone including yourself.

You are rooted and grounded in life.

The world is a safe and loving place.

You are safe in this world.

And when you are ready to start coming out of this meditation, wiggle your fingers and wiggle your toes.

Become aware of your breath.

And when you are ready, you can open your eyes.

Quantum Connection Guided Meditation Transcript

Imagine the space inside your ear canals.

Imagine the space inside your nostrils.

Imagine the space surrounding your head.

Imagine the space surrounding your chest, shoulders, and upper back.

Imagine the space surrounding your abdomen and lower back.

Imagine the space surrounding your pelvis.

Imagine the space surrounding your upper legs.

Imagine the space surrounding your lower legs.

Imagine the space surrounding your feet.

Imagine the space surrounding your entire body.

Imagine the space between you and the front of the room.

Imagine the space between you and the back of the room.

Imagine the space between you and the ceiling.

Now, I want you to go within yourself to the space within your body.

Go deeper into your body into the space between your cells.

Now, go even deeper to the space between the interwoven strands of your DNA.

Here you will see a glowing light representing you as pure energy.

There is a feeling of incredible love here — unconditional love.

Rest in this energy, knowing you are safe here.

Allow yourself to become this energy of unconditional love.

Here, you are timeless and infinite.

Here, you are infinitely powerful.

Now, see yourself as pure energy, expanding outward at the speed of light in all directions.

Merging with the energies of the unified field of divine consciousness.

Where everything becomes the energy of one love.

Here you become unlimited in power with unlimited potential.

Where you have no drama and no sickness.

Where you have no limitations or restrictions.

Here you are an infinite being of unconditional love with infinite potential.

And you know this is you.

This is you as pure energy where you are free to love yourself unconditionally and accept yourself unconditionally.

And in this knowing — in this state of pure energy — you are all powerful.

Where you are one with the divine.

Here all possibilities exist.

This space of infinite potential is always you as pure energy.

You can always access this field of pure energy by going within.

Where there is only pure energy and divine love.

Believe this.

Know this.

It is in this space of pure energy that miracles occur.

So practice going here and becoming comfortable with being the pure energy of unconditional love.

Because this is who you truly are — an unconditionally loving and divine being with infinite potential.

Transmuting Negative Emotions
Guided Meditation Transcript

Find a quiet area, relax into a comfortable position, and close your eyes.

Take a deep, slow breath in, and a relaxed, slow breath out.

Take another deep, slow breath in, and a relaxed, slow breath out.

Take one more deep, slow breath in, and a relaxed, slow breath out.

Think of an ongoing situation or experience that creates a stressful reaction and negative emotion in your body and mind.

Become fully aware of this negative emotion.

Whatever it is, let yourself fully feel this negative emotion.

It's okay to feel it, because part of the process of healing it is to allow yourself to feel it.

Now that you are feeling this negative emotion, become aware of the area you feel it most in your body.

It may be in your head or neck or shoulders, your chest or abdomen, or somewhere else.

Just become aware of the area or areas in your body where you most intensely feel this negative emotion.

Be aware of what this emotion feels like in your body.

Is it tension? Is it a tightness or pressure? Or is it a heavy sensation?

Feel this sensation in your body that's associated with this emotion.

It's okay to feel it, because it won't last.

Now that you have become fully aware of the area in your body in which you feel this negative emotion, start to slowly, but deeply, breathe through this area of your body.

As you continue to breathe, release resistance to feeling this negative emotion and associated sensation.

Imagine the flow of your breath moving in and out of this area of your body.

The intention is to start a flow of energy in this area to help release this emotion.

While being fully aware of this negative emotion and associated bodily sensation, become aware of a bright ball of energy in the center of your heart.

This energy represents the consciousness of your heart mind and contains unconditional love.

Now, see this ball of energy of unconditional love grow brighter and brighter until it takes up the entire space of your heart.

By doing this visualization, you are energizing the consciousness of your heart mind.

Notice how the negative emotion and bodily sensation starts to shift as you energize your heart mind.

Now, set an intention for your heart mind and your subconscious mind to align and tell you the origin of this negative emotion.

You are seeking the original event that created this negative emotion.

This knowing may occur as an epiphany or simply a bubbling up of information from your subconscious mind.

Once you have become aware of this original event for this emotion and the circumstances surrounding it, set the intention for your heart mind to tell you what you need to do to express it, process it, and release it from your body and mind.

This usually involves forgiveness of yourself or someone else.

Continue to allow your heart mind to energize this emotion and bodily sensation with unconditional love and a higher awareness, so that you can process it, and release it.

Continue to slowly breathe in and out as you process the information you are receiving.

And let the wisdom of your heart mind show you how to transmute this negative emotion with love.

<u>Removing Limiting Beliefs</u>
<u>Guided Meditation Transcript</u>

Find a quiet place, relax into a comfortable position, and close your eyes.

Take a deep, slow breath in, and a relaxed, slow breath out.

Take another deep, slow breath in, and a relaxed, slow breath out.

Take one more deep, slow breath in, and a relaxed, slow breath out.

Think of the limiting belief you would like to release and say it to yourself.

Set an intention to see the origin for this limiting belief.

Ask your subconscious mind and higher mind to align to show the answer.

Take a deep, slow breath in, and a relaxed, slow breath out.

Take another deep, slow breath in, and a relaxed, slow breath out.

Take one more deep, slow breath in, and a relaxed, slow breath out.

You are relaxing more and more.

You are feeling very relaxed and very safe.

And you are feeling curious about this limiting belief.

While you think of the limiting belief, scan your body for any areas of resistance.

This resistance may feel like tension, tightness, a heaviness, or a sharp sensation in your body.

Notice the area of your body where you feel the most resistance when you think of the limiting belief.

Now, become aware of the emotion associated with this area of resistance in your body.

Once you recognize the emotion, ask your subconscious mind and higher mind to show you when this emotion and associated limiting belief originated.

Be aware of the first answer that comes to you.

Now, relax, and allow more insight to flow in about the circumstances surrounding this event.

As you continue to relax, allow this information to flow in.

Relax, and more information will come.

Just relax.

Trust this knowing when it feels right.

If this doesn't happen immediately, relax into feeling the emotion associated with the limiting belief, and sit with it.

It may take a little while for all of the information to come in.

As long as you relax into it, and you are ready to see or hear it, your subconscious mind and your higher mind will work in synergy to show this to you.

Now that you know how this limiting belief and its associated emotion originated, ask yourself if you are ready to release it.

If you don't feel ready to release it, that is okay.

Take some time to process this experience.

When you are ready to release it, set an intention to let it go.

You learned something from it and are ready to let it go.

Now that you've set an intention to release the limiting belief, take a deep, slow belly-breath, and visualize blowing this limiting belief and associated emotion out through your heart area and away from your body.

You may need to do this several times as you sense it leaving your body through your heart area.

Take as much time as you need.

This process will be easy if you remember this — it was never the truth in the first place.

When you feel like the limiting belief has gone, set a specific intention or new belief to take its place — a new belief that empowers you on every level of your life.

Your heart mind in conjunction with your subconscious mind has the power to clear limiting beliefs and associated emotions.

Your heart mind is the great healer through the power of unconditional love.

Inner Physician Guided Meditation Transcript

Take a deep, relaxed breath in, and a slow, relaxed breath out.

Take another deep, relaxed breath in, and a slow, relaxed breath out.

Take one more deep, relaxed breath in, and a slow, relaxed breath out.

You are a powerful healer.

Believe that you can heal yourself.

Your body contains an infinitely intelligent inner physician to call on to heal your body.

Your inner physician is made up of all your body's systems and organs, working in perfect harmony.

Ask your body to come into perfect harmony so that your inner physician can heal you right now.

Trust your body to do this with ease.

Take a deep, relaxed breath in, and a slow, relaxed breath out.

You are relaxing more and more, and as you do, your parasympathetic nervous system steps up to assist in recovery, repair, and rejuvenation.

Send love to your brain to assist in processing your healing.

Send love to your immune system to strengthen your immunity.

Send love to your endocrine system to balance your hormones.

Send love to your gastrointestinal tract to optimize your digestion and absorption of your nutrients.

Send love to your lungs to optimize oxygenation and release all grief.

Send love to your liver to optimize detoxification and release all anger.

Send love to your gallbladder to optimize your bile and release all frustration.

Send love to your spleen to strengthen your immune system and release all worry.

Send love to your kidneys to detoxify and cleanse your body and release all fear.

Now, see all of your body's systems and organs being enveloped by a white light of healing energy.

Bathe in this healing energy knowing this divine healing energy, along with your relaxation, trust, and love, is creating harmony throughout your body.

Your body's systems and organs are working together in perfect harmony.

Your body knows exactly what you need.

Your body knows exactly what to do.

Trust that your body can heal and release all doubt.

Now, envision yourself completely healed. In your mind's eye see exactly what you would look like completely healed with perfect health and perfect energy.

Hold that vision of your optimal health, and feel the powerful energy of wholeness — body, mind, and spirit.

Feel what it's like to be completely healthy and whole.

Remember this vision.

Remember this feeling.

This is you.

Trust that.

And as you bring in gratitude for this optimal health and happiness, trust that your body will be healed in divine timing.

You are a powerful being — an infinite and divine being.

You can do all things if you believe.

So believe this. Know this. Trust this.

And then let go of when, where, and how.

Your inner physician loves you and is always working on your behalf to heal you, especially when you believe.

Trust, believe, and relax.

Now, repeat these following words in your mind.

My body's systems and organs are working together in perfect harmony.

I see myself in perfect health.

I feel myself in perfect health.

I am grateful for my perfect health.

Now, continue to see and feel yourself in perfect health, knowing your body and mind are responding to what you see and feel, and especially to what you believe.

Power of the Mind Guided Meditation Transcript

Take a deep, relaxed breath in, and a slow, relaxed breath out.

Take another deep, relaxed breath in, and a slow, relaxed breath out.

Take one more deep, relaxed breath in, and a slow, relaxed breath out.

Say the following words after me, silently in your mind.

"I believe in the power of my mind."

"I trust in the power of my mind."

"I call upon my higher mind… my conscious mind… my heart mind… my subconscious mind… and my DNA mind… to align in full harmony."

Now, listen to my words as you follow my voice.

See a white ball of light in the center of your head — this represents your conscious mind.

Now, see another white ball of light floating three feet above your head — this represents your higher mind.

Now, envision a stream of light coming down from the ball of white light of your higher mind and connecting with the ball of white light of your conscious mind.

And as you see the two connect, you begin to feel love.

This is how you know you are aligned with your higher mind.

It brings a feeling of unconditional love.

This is because your higher mind is a part of divine consciousness.

Now, see a ball of bright white light in the middle of your heart — this represents your heart mind.

See the stream of white light connecting your higher mind and conscious mind extend downward into your heart and connect with this ball of white light — your heart mind.

When all three are connected, you begin to feel even more unconditional love.

Open your heart.

Allow the love in.

And because you have aligned your higher mind to your heart mind, your intuition has increased a thousand fold.

Now, see this stream of white light connecting your higher mind, your conscious mind, and your heart mind start to spread out along all of the nerves of your body, connecting to a white light that is in all of the tissues of your body — this represents your subconscious mind.

And as you align the energies of your consciousness to your subconscious mind, your subconscious mind is purged of all limiting beliefs, because you are bringing in only the truth.

Now, see this vibrating white light of consciousness coming into your body, down through your head, into your heart, and extending into all the tissues of your body. See this energy of white light extending into and connecting with a glowing white light in the chromosomes of your cells — this is your DNA mind.

And as you do, you become aware of an incredible love and wisdom permeating your entire body.

You feel a shift in your body of a higher awareness, and your body begins to feel light, almost as if you could float up into the air.

And as the glow of this vibrating white light of your consciousness extends into your DNA, your body starts to vibrate even stronger, and you feel an even more powerful sense of unconditional love and wisdom.

And in a split second, all of your genes that trigger good health and wellness are turned on, and in a split second, all of your genes that trigger disease are turned off.

And you are healthy, whole, and powerful.

You are a light being.

You are an energy being.

You are an infinite being.

You are now your own authority and will always trust your intuition from this point forward.

You will always listen to your inner voice and trust yourself from now on.

Now, bring in a sense of incredible gratitude for this gift you have given yourself.

Thank yourself.

Honor yourself.

This loving gratitude will keep you aligned, healthy, and strong.

And you will always remember you are a powerful being who can do all things, if you only believe.

Now, become aware of your body as you begin to come back into the room. Wiggle your toes and wiggle your fingers.

Become aware of your breath.

And when you are ready, you can open your eyes.

Appendix 2

Core Positive Affirmations

- I love myself unconditionally.
- I forgive myself unconditionally.
- I accept myself unconditionally.
- I respect myself.
- I trust myself.
- I take care of myself.
- I deserve to be happy.
- I deserve to be loved.
- I am courageous.
- I am consciously living my divine purpose.
- I am one with all creation and with the divine.
- I have faith that all is well.
- I am an energetic and infinite being.
- I am open to the ideas and perspectives of others.
- I learn from my experiences.
- I evaluate myself honestly.

- I can freely and honestly express my thoughts and feelings.
- I communicate clearly and effectively.
- I can speak up for myself.
- I have clear boundaries with others.
- I follow my dreams.
- I say what I mean and mean what I say.
- I feel empowered to achieve whatever I choose.
- I am open to divine and human love.
- Healing energy flows through my body.
- I am comfortable opening my heart and sharing with others.
- I forgive others and release all bitterness.
- I am compassionate toward myself.
- I am compassionate toward others.
- I release all resentments and grudges.
- I accept healing now.
- I trust in the healing power of love.
- My personal power is growing each day.
- I am confident in my abilities.
- I have what it takes to make my way in the world.
- I am creative and creativity flows from me.
- Sexuality is to be enjoyed.
- I celebrate the gift of sexuality.
- I can receive pleasure.
- I release all blame and guilt.
- I release the need to control others.
- The universe is a safe and loving place.

- I am safe in this world.
- Life provides what I need.
- I am rooted and grounded in life.

Appendix 3

<u>Social Learning and Spontaneous Remission Resources:</u>

<u>Clinical Holistic Medicine: Induction of Spontaneous Remission of Cancer by Recovery of the Human Character and the Purpose of Life (the Life Mission)</u>

Ventegodt S, Morad M, Hyam E, Merrick J. Clinical holistic medicine: induction of spontaneous remission of cancer by recovery of the human character and the purpose of life (the life mission). Scientific World Journal. 2004;4:362-77.

Abstract:

The recovery of the human character and purpose of life with consciousness-based medicine seems to be able to induce spontaneous remissions in several diseases. On two different occasions, we observed breast tumors reduced to less than half their original diameters (clinically judged) during a holistic session, when working with the patients in accordance with the holistic process theory of healing, the life mission theory, and the theory of human character. One tumor was histologically diagnosed as malign breast cancer prior to the session, while the other was under examination. As both patients had the affected regions of the breast surgically removed immediately after the session, we are unable to determine if they were actually healed by the holistic treatment. We find it extremely interesting that the size of a tumor can be reduced dramatically within a few hours of holistic treatment, when the patient is highly motivated for personal development. The reduction of tumor size is in accordance with the holistic view that many types of cancer are caused by emotional and existential disturbances. From a holistic perspective, cancer can be understood as a simple disturbance of the cells, arising from the tissue holding on to a trauma with strong emotional content. This is called "a blockage," where the function of the cells is changed from their original function in the tissue to a function of holding emotions. The reduction of the tumor in the two cases happened when old painful emotions were identified in the tissues, in and around the tumor, and processed into understanding; when the patients finally did let go of negative beliefs and attitudes that had kept the feeling(s) repressed to that part of the body, the tumor first softened and then disappeared, presumably by apoptosis. We believe that the consciousness-based/holistic medical toolbox has a serious additional offer to cancer patients, and we will therefore strongly encourage the scientific society to explore these new possibilities. Our holistic medical research meets both ethical dilemmas and practical difficulties, as it obviously is important for the research in induced spontaneous remissions that surgery and chemotherapy is not used before it is absolutely necessary. On the other hand, is it important for the patient's survival that they receive any well-documented treatment as soon as possible. An additional aspect for the patient who is able to cure her own cancer is that she is much less likely to get cancer again and much better prepared to deal with other diseases and challenges in life. Knowing that one can fight even cancer gives a strong belief in life and the need to improve quality of life. The high incidence of secondary cancers and the physical and emotional wounds from the biomedical treatment seem to justify a focus on prevention and additional holistic treatment modules. To support the patient in learning the mastery of coherence of body and life, using the crisis of cancer to recover the human character and the purpose of life, seems turning a personal potential disaster into the greatest gift of all. When it comes down to it, life is not just about surviving; what is more important is to live fully, to learn from the great challenges of life, and to obtain the optimal quality of life while being here.

Lung cancer with spontaneous regression of primary and metastatic sites: A case report

Ogawa R, Watanabe H, Yazaki K, et al. Lung cancer with spontaneous regression of primary and metastatic sites: A case report. Oncol Lett. 2015;10(1):550-552.

Abstract:

Partial or complete spontaneous cancer regression is a rare phenomenon, particularly in patients with lung cancer. This is the case report of a patient with lung cancer who exhibited spontaneous regression of the primary as well as metastatic lesions, without receiving any treatment. Spontaneous regression commenced within a week of obtaining pathological specimens by transbronchial and percutaneous biopsies from the primary lesion and metastatic lymph nodes of the left side of the neck. The reason for this phenomenon is unknown; however, we hypothesized that there may be an immunological association between the stimulus of the biopsies and the spontaneous regression. This patient should be closely followed up to monitor the clinical course of this unusual case.

A Case of Spontaneous Regression of Advanced Colon Cancer

Shimizu H, Kochi M, Kaiga T, Mihara Y, Fujii M, Takayama T. A case of spontaneous regression of advanced colon cancer. Anticancer Res. 2010;30(6):2351-3.

Abstract:

A case of spontaneous regression of colon cancer is reported. The patient, an 80-year-old man, was referred to the hospital in January 2004. Colonoscopy revealed a type 2 tumor in the transverse colon which was diagnosed as an adenocarcinoma. A computed tomography scan also revealed a right renal tumor. Urological examination disclosed renal cell cancer. The patient subsequently refused surgical treatment and did not visit the hospital again for 6 months, during which time he received neither anticancer treatment nor any other medication. Another colonoscopy in August 2004 resulted in reclassification of the tumor to a IIc lesion, and the biopsy was negative for cancer. A right nephrectomy was carried out, and observation was performed for development of colonic lesions. In January 2007, colonoscopy revealed that the IIc lesion had disappeared. The patient was still alive with no sign of recurrence 64 months after disappearance of the lesion. Conclusion: This finding suggests that spontaneous regression can occur in advanced colon cancer.

Notes

1. Yamaguchi M, Deguchi M, Miyazaki Y. The effects of exercise in forest and urban environments on sympathetic nervous activity of normal young adults. J Int Med Res. 2006;34(2):152–9.

2. Li Q, Morimoto K, Nakadai A, et al. Forest bathing enhances human natural killer activity and expression of anticancer proteins. Int J Immunopathol Pharmacol. 2007;20(2 Suppl 2):3–8.

3. Li Q, Morimoto K, Kobayashi M, et al. A forest bathing trip increases human natural killer activity and expression of anticancer proteins in female subjects. J Biol Regul Homeost Agents. 2008;22(1):45–55.

4. Trakhtenberg EC. The effects of guided imagery on the immune system: a critical review. Int J Neurosci. 2008;118(6):839–55.

5. Mccraty R, Zayas MA. Cardiac coherence, self-regulation, autonomic stability, and psychosocial well-being. Front Psychol. 2014;5:1090.

6. Goyal M, Singh S, Sibinga EM, et al. Meditation programs for psychological stress and well-being: a systematic review and meta-analysis. JAMA Intern Med. 2014;174(3):357–68.

7. Bhasin MK, Dusek JA, Chang BH, et al. Relaxation response induces temporal transcriptome changes in energy metabolism, insulin secretion and inflammatory pathways. PLoS ONE. 2013;8(5):e62817.

8. Kaliman P, Alvarez-lópez MJ, Cosín-tomás M, Rosenkranz MA, Lutz A, Davidson RJ. Rapid changes in histone deacetylases and inflammatory gene expression in expert meditators. Psychoneuroendocrinology. 2014;40:96–107.

9. Dusek JA, Otu HH, Wohlhueter AL, et al. Genomic counter-stress changes induced by the relaxation response. PLoS ONE. 2008;3(7):e2576.

10. Bhasin MK, Dusek JA, Chang BH, et al. Relaxation response induces temporal transcriptome changes in energy metabolism, insulin secretion and inflammatory pathways. PLoS ONE. 2013;8(5):e62817.

11. Creswell JD, Irwin MR, Burklund LJ, et al. Mindfulness-Based Stress Reduction training reduces loneliness and proinflammatory gene expression in older adults: a small randomized controlled trial. Brain Behav Immun. 2012;26(7):1095–101.

12. Black DS, Cole SW, Irwin MR, et al. Yogic meditation reverses NF-κB and IRF-related transcriptome dynamics in leukocytes of family dementia caregivers in a randomized controlled trial. Psychoneuroendocrinology. 2013;38(3):348–55.

13. Lazar SW, Kerr CE, Wasserman RH, et al. Meditation experience is associated with increased cortical thickness. Neuroreport. 2005;16(17):1893–7.

14. Luders E, Cherbuin N, Kurth F. Forever Young(er): potential age-defying effects of long-term meditation on gray matter atrophy. Front Psychol. 2014;5:1551.

15. Pascual-leone A, Nguyet D, Cohen LG, Brasil-neto JP, Cammarota A, Hallett M. Modulation of muscle responses evoked by transcranial magnetic stimulation during the acquisition of new fine motor skills. J Neurophysiol. 1995;74(3):1037–45.

16. Ranganathan VK, Siemionow V, Liu JZ, Sahgal V, Yue GH. From mental power to muscle power — gaining strength by using the mind. Neuropsychologia. 2004;42(7):944–56.

17. Ridderinkhof KR, Brass M. How Kinesthetic Motor Imagery works: a predictive-processing theory of visualization in sports and motor expertise. J Physiol Paris. 2015;109(1–3):53–63.

18. Khansari N, Shakiba Y, Mahmoudi M. Chronic inflammation and oxidative stress as a major cause of age-related diseases and cancer. Recent Pat Inflamm Allergy Drug Discov. 2009;3(1):73–80.

19. Gao HM, Hong JS. Why neurodegenerative diseases are progressive: uncontrolled inflammation drives disease progression. Trends Immunol. 2008;29(8):357–65.

20. Xu H, Barnes GT, Yang Q, et al. Chronic inflammation in fat plays a crucial role in the development of obesity-related insulin resistance. J Clin Invest. 2003;112(12):1821–30.

21. Barnes PJ, Karin M. Nuclear factor-kappaB: a pivotal transcription factor in chronic inflammatory diseases. N Engl J Med. 1997;336(15):1066–71.

22. Murakami M, Hirano T. The molecular mechanisms of chronic inflammation development. Front Immunol. 2012;3:323.

23. Lindqvist PG, Epstein E, Nielsen K, Landin-olsson M, Ingvar C, Olsson H. Avoidance of sun exposure as a risk factor for major causes of death: a competing risk analysis of the Melanoma in Southern Sweden cohort. J Intern Med. 2016; Mar 16. doi: 10.1111/joim.12496. [Epub ahead of print]

24. Peterlik M. Vitamin D insufficiency and chronic diseases: hype and reality. Food Funct. 2012;3(8):784–94.

25. Oschman JL, Chevalier G, Brown R. The effects of grounding (earthing) on inflammation, the immune response, wound healing, and prevention and treatment of chronic inflammatory and autoimmune diseases. J Inflamm Res. 2015;8:83–96.

26. Xie L, Kang H, Xu Q, et al. Sleep drives metabolite clearance from the adult brain. Science. 2013;342(6156):373–7.

27. Hedendahl L, Carlberg M, Hardell L. Electromagnetic hypersensitivity — an increasing challenge to the medical profession. Rev Environ Health. 2015;30(4):209–15

28. Czeisler CA. Perspective: casting light on sleep deficiency. Nature. 2013;497(7450):S13.

29. Chakravorty S, Jackson N, Chaudhary N, et al. Daytime sleepiness: associations with alcohol use and sleep duration in Americans. Sleep Disord. 2014;2014:959152.

30. O'laoire S. An experimental study of the effects of distant, intercessory prayer on self-esteem, anxiety, and depression. Altern Ther Health Med. 1997;3(6)38–53.

31. Olver IN, Dutney A. A randomized, blinded study of the impact of intercessory prayer on spiritual well-being in patients with cancer. Altern Ther Health Med. 2012;18(5):18–27.

32. Ludtke R. [A randomized, controlled trial of the effects of remote, intercessory prayer on outcomes in patients admitted to the coronary care unit. Arch Intern Med 1999; 159:2273-2278]. Forsch Komplementarmed Klass Naturheilkd. 2000;7(3):161–2.

33. Ransom SM, Stairs IH, Archibald AM, et al. A millisecond pulsar in a stellar triple system. Nature. 2014; Jan 5. doi: 10.1038/nature12917. [Epub ahead of print]

34. Mccraty R, Deyhle A, Childre D. The global coherence initiative: creating a coherent planetary standing wave. Glob Adv Health Med. 2012;1(1):64–77.

35. Rudd R. The Gene Keys, Unlocking the Higher Purpose Hidden in Your DNA. Watkins Pub Limited; 2013.

36. Mihelic, F. Matthew. Model of Biological Quantum Logic in DNA. Life. 2013;3(3):474.

37. Giustina M, Mech A, Ramelow S, et al. Bell violation using entangled photons without the fair-sampling assumption. Nature. 2013;497(7448):227–30.

38. Available at: http://arxiv.org/abs/1303.0614. Accessed January 28, 2014.

39. Dusek JA, Otu HH, Wohlhueter AL, et al. Genomic counter-stress changes induced by the relaxation response. PLoS ONE. 2008;3(7):e2576.

40. Mccraty R, Atkinson M, Bradley RT. Electrophysiological evidence of intuition: Part 2. A system-wide process?. J Altern Complement Med. 2004;10(2):325–36.

41. Mandelbrot BB. The Fractal Geometry of Nature. Macmillan; 1983.

42. Mcnally JG, Mazza D. Fractal geometry in the nucleus. EMBO J. 2010;29(1):2–3.

43. Di ieva A, Grizzi F, Jelinek H, Pellionisz AJ, Losa GA. Fractals in the Neurosciences, Part I: General Principles and Basic Neurosciences. Neuroscientist. 2013; Dec 20

44. Yamamoto Y, Fortrat JO, Hughson RL. On the fractal nature of heart rate variability in humans: effects of respiratory sinus arrhythmia. Am J Physiol. 1995;269(2 Pt 2):H480–6.

45. The Energetic Heart: GCI Edition. Institute of Heartmath; 2003. https://www.heartmath.org/assets/uploads/2015/02/the-energetic-heart-gci-edition.pdf. Accessed April 9, 2016.

46. Stroink G. Principles of cardiomagnetism. In: Williamson SJ, Hoke M, Stroink G, Kotani M, eds. Advances in Biomag-netism. New York: Plenum Press, 1989:47–57

47. Bradley RT, Mccraty R, Atkinson M, Tomasino D, Daugherty A, Arguelles L. Emotion self-regulation, psychophysiological coherence, and test anxiety: results from an experiment using electrophysiological measures. Appl Psychophysiol Biofeedback. 2010;35(4):261–83.

48. Mccraty R, Atkinson M, Bradley RT. Electrophysiological evidence of intuition: part 1. The surprising role of the heart. J Altern Complement Med. 2004;10(1):133–43.

49. Mccraty R, Atkinson M, Bradley RT. Electrophysiological evidence of intuition: Part 2. A system-wide process?. J Altern Complement Med. 2004;10(2):325–36.

50. Herman DB, Susser ES, Struening EL, Link BL. Adverse childhood experiences: are they risk factors for adult homelessness?. Am J Public Health. 1997;87(2):249–55.

51. Moon C, Lagercrantz H, Kuhl PK. Language experienced in utero affects vowel perception after birth: a two-country study. Acta Paediatr. 2013;102(2):156–60.

52. Lutz A, Greischar LL, Rawlings NB, Ricard M, Davidson RJ. Long-term meditators self-induce high-amplitude gamma synchrony during mental practice. Proc Natl Acad Sci USA. 2004;101(46):16369–73.

53. Huang TL, Charyton C. A comprehensive review of the psychological effects of brainwave entrainment. Altern Ther Health Med. 2008;14(5):38–50.

54. Zampi DD. Efficacy of Theta Binaural Beats for the Treatment of Chronic Pain. Altern Ther Health Med. 2016;22(1):32–8.

55. Moseley JB, O'malley K, Petersen NJ, et al. A controlled trial of arthroscopic surgery for osteoarthritis of the knee. N Engl J Med. 2002;347(2):81–8.

56. Kam-hansen S, Jakubowski M, Kelley JM, et al. Altered placebo and drug labeling changes the outcome of episodic migraine attacks. Sci Transl Med. 2014;6(218):218ra5.

57. Goebel MU, Trebst AE, Steiner J, et al. Behavioral conditioning of immunosuppression is possible in humans. FASEB J. 2002;16(14):1869–73.

58. De la fuente-fernández R, Ruth TJ, Sossi V, Schulzer M, Calne DB, Stoessl AJ. Expectation and dopamine release: mechanism of the placebo effect in Parkinson's disease. Science. 2001;293(5532):1164-6.

59. Goetz CG, Wuu J, Mcdermott MP, et al. Placebo response in Parkinson's disease: comparisons among 11 trials covering medical and surgical interventions. Mov Disord. 2008;23(5):690-9.

60. Benedetti F, Carlino E, Pollo A. How placebos change the patient's brain. Neuropsychopharmacology. 2011;36(1):339-54.

61. Colloca L, Benedetti F. Placebo analgesia induced by social observational learning. Pain. 2009;144(1-2):28-34.

62. Geers AL, Wellman JA, Fowler SL, Helfer SG, France CR. Dispositional optimism predicts placebo analgesia. J Pain. 2010;11(11):1165-71.

63. Geers AL, Helfer SG, Kosbab K, Weiland PE, Landry SJ. Reconsidering the role of personality in placebo effects: dispositional optimism, situational expectations, and the placebo response. J Psychosom Res. 2005;58(2):121-7.

CPSIA information can be obtained
at www.ICGtesting.com
Printed in the USA
BVHW030910300922
648379BV00014B/472